Carb Cycling Meal Prep Cookbook

1000 Days Flavorful and Easy-to-Follow Recipes for Beginners to keep Your Body Healthy with Carb Cycling Diet

Stameria Racia

© Copyright 2023 Stameria Racia - All Rights Reserved.

It is in no way legal to reproduce, duplicate, or transmit any part of this document by either electronic means or in printed format. Recording of this publication is strictly prohibited, and any storage of this material is not allowed unless with written permission from the publisher. All rights reserved.

The information provided herein is stated to be truthful and consistent, in that any liability, regarding inattention or otherwise, by any usage or abuse of any policies, processes, or directions contained within is the solitary and complete responsibility of the recipient reader. Under no circumstances will any legal liability or blame be held against the publisher for any reparation, damages, or monetary loss due to the information herein, either directly or indirectly.

Respective authors own all copyrights not held by the publisher.

Legal Notice:

This book is copyright protected. This is only for personal use. You cannot amend, distribute, sell, use, quote or paraphrase any part of the content within this book without the consent of the author or copyright owner. Legal action will be pursued if this is breached.

Disclaimer Notice:

Please note the information contained within this document is for educational and entertainment purposes only. Every attempt has been made to provide accurate, up-to-date, reliable, and complete information. No warranties of any kind are expressed or implied. Readers acknowledge that the author is not engaging in the rendering of legal, financial, medical or professional advice.

By reading this document, the reader agrees that under no circumstances are we responsible for any losses, direct or indirect, which are incurred as a result of the use of information contained within this document, including, but not limited to, errors, omissions, or inaccuracies.

Table of Contents

INTRODUCTION

What is Carb Cycling?

Carb cycling is a dietary approach that involves varying your carbohydrate intake on a daily, weekly, or monthly basis. It is commonly used by athletes, bodybuilders, and fitness enthusiasts to optimize performance, manage body composition, and improve metabolic flexibility.

The principle of carb cycling involves strategically manipulating your carbohydrate intake based on specific goals and individual needs. While the specific structure of carb cycling can vary, the underlying principles typically involve the following:

- Cycling between high, low, and moderate-carb days: Carb cycling involves alternating between days with higher carbohydrate intake (high-carb days), days with lower carbohydrate intake (low-carb days), and days with a moderate carbohydrate intake (moderate-carb days).

- Timing carbohydrate intake around activity levels: The distribution of high, low, and moderate-carb days can be based on your activity levels. High-carb days are often scheduled on days with intense workouts or physical activities that require increased energy. Low-carb days may be scheduled on rest days or days with light physical activity. Moderate-carb days can be scheduled on days with moderate exercise or training.

- Adjusting macronutrient intake: Along with varying carbohydrate intake, individuals may also adjust their fat and protein intake accordingly. While carbohydrate intake is manipulated, it's important to maintain adequate protein intake to support muscle maintenance and repair.

- Individualization: The structure and duration of carb cycling can vary based on individual goals, body composition, activity levels, metabolic factors, and personal preferences. It's important to tailor the approach

to meet your specific needs and consult with a healthcare professional or registered dietitian for personalized guidance.

- Tracking and monitoring: Keeping track of your carbohydrate intake, as well as other macronutrients, can be helpful in implementing carb cycling effectively. This can be done through food diaries, tracking apps, or working with a nutritionist to ensure you're meeting your macronutrient goals.

- Adjusting based on feedback: It's important to listen to your body and adjust your carb cycling approach based on how you feel and the results you're experiencing. Monitoring factors such as energy levels, performance, body composition changes, and overall well-being can help you make necessary adjustments to optimize the approach.

Remember that carb cycling is a flexible approach, and there is no one-size-fits-all method. It can be customized to align with your goals, preferences, and lifestyle. Working with a healthcare professional or registered dietitian can provide personalized guidance and help you develop an appropriate carb cycling plan that suits your individual needs.

Benefits of Carb Cycling

Carb cycling offers several potential benefits. Here are some of the key advantages associated with this dietary approach:

- Fat loss: Carb cycling can be an effective strategy for promoting fat loss. By cycling between low-carb and high-carb days, the body can utilize stored fat as an energy source during low-carb days while replenishing glycogen stores on high-carb days. This can create a calorie deficit, leading to weight loss and improved body composition.

- Muscle preservation: When following a calorie-restricted diet for fat loss, there is a risk of losing muscle mass along with fat. By incorporating high-carb days into the plan, carb cycling can help preserve muscle glycogen stores, supporting muscle recovery and minimizing muscle breakdown.

- Enhanced athletic performance: Carbohydrates are the body's primary source of energy for high-intensity exercise. By strategically timing high-carb days around intense workouts or competitions, carb cycling can provide the necessary glycogen stores to fuel performance, improving endurance and power output.

- Improved metabolic flexibility: Consistently consuming a high-carbohydrate diet can lead to a reliance on carbohydrates as the primary fuel source. Carb cycling encourages the body to become more metabolically flexible by switching between carbohydrate and fat metabolism. This adaptability can enhance overall metabolic health.

- Hormonal regulation: Carbohydrate intake influences the production and release of various hormones, including insulin, leptin, and ghrelin. Carb cycling can help regulate these hormones, optimizing metabolism, hunger, satiety, and energy balance.

- Flexibility and sustainability: One of the benefits of carb cycling is its flexibility compared to strict, low-carb diets. It allows for the inclusion of higher-carb meals or days, which can make the diet more enjoyable and easier to stick to in the long term. This flexibility can improve adherence and overall dietary sustainability.

- Psychological benefits: Carb cycling can provide psychological relief for individuals who struggle with the strictness of conventional diets. Having structured high-carb days can help alleviate cravings, reduce feelings of deprivation, and promote a healthier relationship with food.

- Muscle fullness and vascularity: On high-carb days, glycogen replenishment can lead to increased muscle fullness and vascularity, giving a more visually appealing appearance.

It's worth noting that the specific benefits of carb cycling can vary among individuals, depending on factors such as activity levels, metabolic rate, body composition, and overall health. Additionally, it's important to tailor the approach to individual goals and preferences, seeking guidance from a healthcare professional or registered dietitian for personalized advice.

Disadvantages of Carb Cycling

While carb cycling can have several benefits, there are also some potential disadvantages or considerations to keep in mind. These include:

- Complexity: Carb cycling can be more complex than following a consistent macronutrient distribution. It requires planning and tracking carbohydrate intake on different days, which may be challenging for some individuals.

- Individual variation: Carb cycling is not a one-size-fits-all approach. The specific structure and timing of carb cycling may need to be tailored to an individual's goals, activity levels, and metabolic factors. It may require experimentation and adjustments to find the optimal carb cycling plan for each person.

- Potential for inconsistent energy levels: On low-carb days, individuals may experience lower energy levels due to reduced carbohydrate availability. This can impact performance and overall well-being, particularly for those engaging in intense physical activity. However, proper adjustment and nutrient timing can help mitigate this issue.

- Psychological challenges: Carb cycling can be mentally challenging for some individuals, particularly those who struggle with strict diet rules or have a history of disordered eating. The alternating nature of carb cycling may lead to feelings of restriction or frustration. It's important to consider your relationship with food and ensure that carb cycling aligns with your overall well-being.

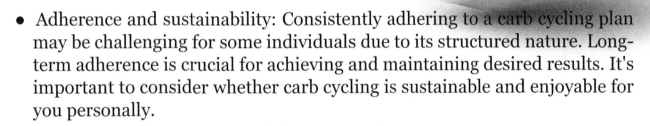

- Potential for overcompensation: On high-carb days, there is a risk of overcompensating by consuming excessive calories or indulging in unhealthy food choices. It's important to maintain a balanced and nutritious diet even on high-carb days to support overall health and prevent negative effects on body composition.

- Adherence and sustainability: Consistently adhering to a carb cycling plan may be challenging for some individuals due to its structured nature. Long-term adherence is crucial for achieving and maintaining desired results. It's important to consider whether carb cycling is sustainable and enjoyable for you personally.

- Individual response: As with any dietary approach, individual responses can vary. While carb cycling may work well for some individuals, others may not experience the desired benefits or find it effective for their goals. It's important to monitor your progress, assess how your body responds, and make adjustments as needed.

It's advisable to consult with a healthcare professional or registered dietitian to discuss your specific circumstances and goals. They can provide personalized guidance, evaluate potential disadvantages, and help you make an informed decision about whether carb cycling is suitable for you.

Is Carb Cycling Right for Me?

Determining whether carb cycling is right for you depends on several factors, including your goals, current health status, activity levels, and personal preferences. Here are some points to consider when deciding if carb cycling is a suitable approach for you:

- Goals: Carb cycling is commonly used for goals such as fat loss, muscle gain, athletic performance enhancement, and metabolic flexibility. If your goals align with these outcomes, carb cycling may be worth exploring.

- Activity levels: Carb cycling is often beneficial for individuals who engage in regular physical activity, particularly high-intensity workouts or endurance training. Timing higher carbohydrate intake around exercise sessions can provide the necessary energy for performance and recovery.

- Metabolic factors: If you have good metabolic flexibility and can easily switch between utilizing carbohydrates and fats for energy, carb cycling may be a suitable option. However, individuals with certain metabolic conditions, such as diabetes, insulin resistance, or metabolic syndrome, may need to approach carb cycling with caution or seek guidance from a healthcare professional.

- Dietary adherence: Carb cycling can provide some flexibility in your diet compared to strict, low-carb approaches. If you find it challenging to adhere to restrictive diets for extended periods, carb cycling might be a more sustainable option for you.

- Personal preferences: Some individuals simply prefer the flexibility and variety offered by carb cycling. If you enjoy having higher-carb days to satisfy cravings or prefer the mental and physical benefits associated with cycling your carbohydrate intake, it may be a suitable approach for you.

It's important to note that carb cycling is not the only effective approach to nutrition and achieving your goals. Other dietary strategies, such as balanced macronutrient intake, intermittent fasting, or specific eating plans, may also suit your needs. It can be beneficial to consult with a healthcare professional or registered dietitian who can evaluate your specific circumstances and provide personalized advice based on your goals, health status, and preferences. They can help determine if carb cycling aligns with your needs or suggest alternative approaches that may be more appropriate for you.

Is Carb Cycling the Same as No Carb Diet?

No, carb cycling and a no-carb diet (also known as a ketogenic diet) are not the same.

Carb cycling involves alternating between high, low, and moderate carbohydrate intake days, strategically timing carbohydrate consumption based on activity levels and goals. The goal of carb cycling is to optimize performance, body composition, and metabolic flexibility. It allows for periods of higher carbohydrate intake to replenish glycogen stores and support high-intensity workouts, while also incorporating periods of lower carbohydrate intake to promote fat burning and metabolic adaptation.

On the other hand, a no-carb diet, such as a ketogenic diet, is an extremely low-carbohydrate eating plan where carbohydrates are severely restricted, usually to less than 50 grams per day. The primary goal of a ketogenic diet is to induce a state of ketosis, where the body primarily burns fat for fuel instead of carbohydrates. The diet is high in fats, moderate in protein, and very low in carbohydrates. This can lead to increased production of ketones, which are used as an alternative fuel source by the body and the brain.

While both carb cycling and a no-carb diet involve manipulating carbohydrate intake, they have distinct approaches and purposes. Carb cycling offers flexibility and a more balanced macronutrient approach, while a no-carb diet is highly restrictive and focuses on inducing ketosis.

It's important to note that both approaches have their own benefits and considerations, and the choice between them depends on individual goals, preferences, and health factors. Consulting with a healthcare professional or registered dietitian can help you determine which approach aligns best with your needs and helps you achieve your specific goals.

Chapter 1: Breakfast

Low Carb Spinach and Feta Egg Muffins

Prep Time: 10 mins
Cook Time: 20 mins
Servings: 6

Ingredients:

- 6 large eggs
- 1/2 cup spinach, chopped
- 1/4 cup crumbled feta cheese
- 1/4 cup diced red bell pepper
- 1/4 cup diced onion
- Salt and pepper to taste

Directions:

1. Preheat the oven to 350°F. Grease a muffin tin or line with paper liners.
2. In a bowl, whisk the eggs until well beaten. Season with salt and pepper.
3. Add the chopped spinach, feta cheese, diced red bell pepper, and diced onion to the bowl. Stir to combine.
4. Pour the egg mixture evenly into the prepared muffin tin, filling each cup about three-quarters full.
5. Bake in the preheated oven for 18-20 minutes or until the eggs are set and the tops are lightly golden.
6. Remove from the oven and let cool for a few minutes before removing the egg muffins from the tin. Serve warm or refrigerate for meal prep.

Nutritional Value (Amount per Serving):

Calories: 78; Protein: 3.9; Fat: 5.88; Carbs: 2.35

Low Carb Breakfast Casserole

Prep Time: 15 mins
Cook Time: 40 mins
Servings: 8

Ingredients:

- 12 large eggs
- 1/2 cup heavy cream
- 1 cup shredded cheddar cheese
- 1 cup diced ham
- 1/2 cup diced bell peppers
- 1/2 cup diced onions
- Salt and pepper to taste

Directions:

1. Preheat the oven to 375°F. Grease a 9x13-inch baking dish.
2. In a large bowl, whisk together the eggs and heavy cream. Season with salt and pepper.
3. Add the shredded cheddar cheese, diced ham, diced bell peppers, and diced onions to the bowl. Stir to combine.
4. Pour the egg mixture into the prepared baking dish, spreading it evenly.
5. Bake in the preheated oven for 35-40 minutes or until the eggs are set and the top is golden brown.
6. Remove from the oven and let cool for a few minutes before slicing into squares. Serve warm or refrigerate for meal prep.

Nutritional Value (Amount per Serving):

Calories: 114; Protein: 4.45; Fat: 9.57; Carbs: 2.59

Low Carb Breakfast Burrito

Prep Time: 10 mins
Cook Time: 15 mins
Servings: 4

Ingredients:

- 4 large eggs
- 4 low-carb tortillas
- 1/2 cup shredded cheddar cheese
- 1/4 cup diced tomatoes
- 1/4 cup diced bell peppers
- 1/4 cup diced onions
- 4 slices cooked bacon, crumbled
- Salt and pepper to taste
- Salsa and sour cream for serving

Directions:

1. In a bowl, whisk the eggs until well beaten. Season with salt and pepper.
2. Heat a non-stick skillet over medium heat. Pour the beaten eggs into the skillet and cook, stirring occasionally, until scrambled and cooked through.
3. Warm the low-carb tortillas in a separate skillet or microwave.
4. Divide the scrambled eggs evenly among the tortillas, placing them in the center.
5. Sprinkle shredded cheddar cheese, diced tomatoes, diced bell peppers, diced onions, and crumbled bacon over the eggs.
6. Fold the sides of the tortillas over the filling, then roll them up tightly to form burritos.
7. Serve the breakfast burritos with salsa and sour cream on the side.

Nutritional Value (Amount per Serving):

Calories: 171; Protein: 6.4; Fat: 14.78; Carbs: 3.19

Low Carb Chia Pudding

Prep Time: 5 mins
Chill Time: 4 hours
Servings: 2

Ingredients:

- 1 cup unsweetened almond milk
- 1/4 cup chia seeds
- 2 tablespoons low-carb sweetener (e.g., stevia, erythritol)
- 1/2 teaspoon vanilla extract
- Fresh berries for topping

Directions:

1. In a bowl, whisk together the almond milk, chia seeds, low-carb sweetener, and vanilla extract until well combined.
2. Let the mixture sit for 5 minutes, then whisk again to prevent clumping.
3. Cover the bowl and refrigerate for at least 4 hours or overnight, allowing the chia seeds to absorb the liquid and thicken the pudding.
4. Stir the chia pudding before serving to ensure a smooth consistency.
5. Divide the chia pudding into serving bowls or glasses and top with fresh berries. Enjoy chilled.

Nutritional Value (Amount per Serving):

Calories: 78; Protein: 3.84; Fat: 3.99; Carbs: 5.98

Low Carb Greek Yogurt Parfait

Prep Time: 5 mins
Total Time: 10 mins
Servings: 2

Ingredients:

- 1 cup plain Greek yogurt
- 1/4 cup low-carb granola
- 1/4 cup mixed berries (e.g., blueberries, strawberries, raspberries)
- 2 tablespoons chopped nuts (e.g., almonds, walnuts)
- 1 tablespoon sugar-free honey or low-carb sweetener (optional)

Directions:

1. In two serving glasses or bowls, layer the plain Greek yogurt, low-carb granola, mixed berries, and chopped nuts.
2. Repeat the layers until all the ingredients are used, ending with a sprinkle of granola and nuts on top.
3. Drizzle sugar-free honey or sprinkle a low-carb sweetener over the parfait if desired.
4. Serve immediately or refrigerate for later consumption. Enjoy!

Nutritional Value (Amount per Serving):

Calories: 124; Protein: 6; Fat: 7.51; Carbs: 9.08

High Carb Blueberry Pancakes

Prep Time: 10 mins
Cook Time: 15 mins
Servings: 4

Ingredients:

- 1 1/2 cups all-purpose flour
- 2 tablespoons granulated sugar
- 2 teaspoons baking powder
- 1/2 teaspoon salt
- 1 cup milk
- 1 large egg
- 2 tablespoons unsalted butter, melted
- 1 cup fresh blueberries

Directions:

1. In a large bowl, whisk together the flour, sugar, baking powder, and salt.
2. In a separate bowl, whisk together the milk, egg, and melted butter.
3. Pour the wet ingredients into the dry ingredients and stir until just combined. Be careful not to overmix; a few lumps are okay.
4. Gently fold in the fresh blueberries.
5. Heat a non-stick skillet or griddle over medium heat and lightly grease with butter or cooking spray.
6. Pour 1/4 cup of batter onto the skillet for each pancake. Cook until bubbles form on the surface, then flip and cook for an additional 1-2 minutes or until golden brown.
7. Repeat with the remaining batter.
8. Serve the blueberry pancakes warm with maple syrup or your favorite toppings.

Nutritional Value (Amount per Serving):

Calories: 328; Protein: 8.08; Fat: 7.65; Carbs: 56.95

High Carb Cinnamon French Toast

Prep Time: 10 mins
Cook Time: 10 mins
Servings: 4

Ingredients:

- 4 large eggs
- 1/2 cup milk
- 1 teaspoon vanilla extract
- 1 teaspoon ground cinnamon
- 8 slices of bread
- Butter for cooking
- Maple syrup and powdered sugar for serving

Directions:

1. In a shallow bowl, whisk together the eggs, milk, vanilla extract, and ground cinnamon.
2. Dip each slice of bread into the egg mixture, allowing it to soak for a few seconds on each side.
3. Heat a large non-stick skillet or griddle over medium heat and melt a pat of butter.
4. Place the soaked bread slices onto the skillet and cook for 2-3 minutes on each side or until golden brown and crispy.
5. Repeat with the remaining bread slices, adding more butter as needed.
6. Serve the cinnamon French toast warm with maple syrup and a dusting of powdered sugar.

Nutritional Value (Amount per Serving):

Calories: 238; Protein: 7.23; Fat: 6.86; Carbs: 36.4

High Carb Oatmeal with Berries

Prep Time: 5 mins
Cook Time: 5 mins
Servings: 2

Ingredients:

- 1 cup rolled oats
- 2 cups water
- Pinch of salt
- 1/2 cup mixed berries (e.g., strawberries, blueberries, raspberries)
- 2 tablespoons honey or maple syrup
- 2 tablespoons chopped nuts (e.g., almonds, walnuts)

Directions:

1. In a saucepan, bring the water to a boil. Add the rolled oats and salt, then reduce the heat to low.
2. Cook the oats according to the package instructions, usually for about 5 minutes or until they reach your desired consistency, stirring occasionally.
3. Remove the saucepan from the heat and let the oatmeal sit for a minute.
4. Divide the cooked oatmeal into serving bowls and top with mixed berries.
5. Drizzle honey or maple syrup over the oatmeal and sprinkle with chopped nuts.
6. Serve the oatmeal warm and enjoy.

Nutritional Value (Amount per Serving):

Calories: 211; Protein: 9.7; Fat: 6.81; Carbs: 46.65

High Carb Banana Pancakes

Prep Time: 10 mins
Cook Time: 15 mins
Servings: 4

Ingredients:

- 2 ripe bananas, mashed
- 2 large eggs
- 1 cup all-purpose flour
- 1 tablespoon granulated sugar
- 1 teaspoon baking powder
- 1/2 teaspoon salt
- 1/2 cup milk
- 1 teaspoon vanilla extract
- Butter for cooking
- Sliced bananas and maple syrup for serving

Directions:

1. In a large bowl, combine the mashed bananas and eggs. Mix well.
2. Add the flour, sugar, baking powder, salt, milk, and vanilla extract to the bowl. Stir until just combined. The batter may be slightly lumpy.
3. Heat a non-stick skillet or griddle over medium heat and melt a pat of butter.
4. Pour 1/4 cup of batter onto the skillet for each pancake. Cook until bubbles form on the surface, then flip and cook for an additional 1-2 minutes or until golden brown.
5. Repeat with the remaining batter.
6. Serve the banana pancakes warm with sliced bananas and maple syrup.

Nutritional Value (Amount per Serving):

Calories: 224; Protein: 5.55; Fat: 3.57; Carbs: 41.65

High Carb Breakfast Burrito

Prep Time: 10 mins
Cook Time: 15 mins
Servings: 4

Ingredients:

- 4 large eggs
- 4 large flour tortillas
- 1 cup cooked white rice
- 1 cup canned black beans, drained and rinsed
- 1/2 cup shredded cheddar cheese
- 1/4 cup diced tomatoes
- 1/4 cup diced bell peppers
- 1/4 cup diced onions
- Salt and pepper to taste
- Salsa and sour cream for serving

Directions:

1. In a bowl, whisk the eggs until well beaten. Season with salt and pepper.
2. Heat a non-stick skillet over medium heat. Pour the beaten eggs into the skillet and cook, stirring occasionally, until scrambled and cooked through.
3. Warm the flour tortillas in a separate skillet or microwave.
4. Divide the cooked white rice, black beans, scrambled eggs, shredded cheddar cheese, diced tomatoes, diced bell peppers, and diced onions evenly among the tortillas, placing them in the center.
5. Fold the sides of the tortillas over the filling, then roll them up tightly to form burritos.
6. Serve the breakfast burritos with salsa and sour cream on the side.

Nutritional Value (Amount per Serving):

Calories: 311; Protein: 11.74; Fat: 7.67; Carbs: 48.35

Oatmeal Cottage Cheese Waffles

Prep Time: 5 min
Cook Time: 20 min
Servings: 4 (1 waffle each)

Ingredients:

- 4 large eggs
- 2 cups low-fat cottage cheese
- 2 tbsp ground flaxseed
- 1/4 cup water
- 2 cups rolled oats
- 1/2 tsp vanilla or almond extract

Directions:

1. Place all ingredients listed above in a blender and blend until evenly mixed and smooth.
2. Heat a waffle iron.
3. Lightly coat with oil or spray with non-stick spray. Place a heaping 1/2 cup of batter onto the waffle iron and cook 4–5 minutes until golden brown and crisp.
4. Repeat with remaining batter. You should have 4 waffles at the end.

Nutritional Value (Amount per Serving):

Calories: 406; Protein: 30.38; Fat: 24.24; Carbs: 33.75

Chapter 2:
Grains & Beans

Spicy Black Bean Burrito Bowl

Prep Time: 15 mins
Cook Time: 25 mins
Servings: 4

Ingredients:

- 1 cup brown ric
- 1 cup corn kernels
- 1 red bell pepper, diced
- 1 jalapeno pepper, seeded and minced
- 1/2 red onion, diced
- 2 cloves garlic, minced
- 1 teaspoon chili powder
- 1/2 teaspoon cumin
- 1/2 teaspoon paprika
- Salt and pepper to taste
- 1 lime, juiced
- Fresh cilantro, chopped (for garnish)
- 1 can black beans, drained and rinsed

Directions:

1. Cook the brown rice according to package instructions.
2. In a large skillet, heat some oil over medium heat. Add the red onion, garlic, red bell pepper, and jalapeno pepper. Cook until the vegetables are softened, about 5 minutes.
3. Add the black beans, corn kernels, chili powder, cumin, paprika, salt, and pepper to the skillet. Stir well to combine and cook for another 5 minutes.
4. Add the cooked brown rice to the skillet and mix everything together. Cook for an additional 5 minutes to heat through.
5. Remove from heat and drizzle with lime juice. Stir well.
6. Serve the spicy black bean mixture in bowls and garnish with fresh cilantro. Enjoy!

Nutritional Value (Amount per Serving):

Calories: 54; Protein: 1.91; Fat: 0.88; Carbs: 11.85

Quinoa and Chickpea

Prep Time: 15 mins
Cook Time: 20 mins
Servings: 6

Ingredients:

- 1 cup quinoa
- 1 can chickpeas, drained and rinsed
- 1 cup cucumber, diced
- 1 cup cherry tomatoes, halved
- 1/2 cup red onion, diced
- 1/4 cup fresh parsley, chopped
- 1/4 cup fresh mint, chopped
- 1/4 cup olive oil
- 2 tablespoons lemon juice
- 1 clove garlic, minced
- Salt and pepper to taste

Directions:

1. Rinse the quinoa thoroughly under cold water. In a medium saucepan, bring 2 cups of water to a boil. Add the quinoa and reduce the heat to low. Cover and simmer for about 15-20 minutes, or until the quinoa is cooked and the water is absorbed. Fluff with a fork and let it cool.
2. In a large bowl, combine the cooked quinoa, chickpeas, cucumber, cherry tomatoes, red onion, parsley, and mint.
3. In a small bowl, whisk together the olive oil, lemon juice, garlic, salt, and pepper. Pour the dressing over the quinoa mixture and toss to combine.
4. Adjust the seasoning if needed. Serve the quinoa and chickpea chilled or at room temperature. Enjoy!

Nutritional Value (Amount per Serving):

Calories: 283; Protein: 9.47; Fat: 12.62; Carbs: 34.2

Lentil Curry with Basmati Rice

Prep Time: 15 mins
Cook Time: 40 mins
Servings: 4

Ingredients:

- 1 cup dried red lentils
- 1 cup basmati rice
- 1 onion, chopped
- 1 tablespoon ginger, grated
- 1 tablespoon curry powder
- 1 teaspoon cumin
- 1 teaspoon turmeric
- 1/2 teaspoon paprika
- 1 can coconut milk
- 1 can diced tomatoes
- 1 cup vegetable broth
- Salt and pepper to taste
- Fresh cilantro, chopped (for garnish)

Directions:

1. Rinse the red lentils under cold water. In a large saucepan, bring 2 cups of water to a boil. Add the lentils and cook for about 15-20 minutes, or until tender. Drain and set aside.
2. In a separate saucepan, cook the basmati rice according to package instructions.
3. In a large skillet, heat some oil over medium heat. Add the onion, garlic, and ginger. Cook until the onion is translucent, about 5 minutes.
4. Add the curry powder, cumin, turmeric, paprika, salt, and pepper to the skillet. Stir well to coat the onions and spices.
5. Add the cooked lentils, coconut milk, diced tomatoes, and vegetable broth to the skillet. Bring to a simmer and let it cook for about 15 minutes, stirring occasionally.
6. Adjust the seasoning if needed. Serve the lentil curry over the basmati rice and garnish with fresh cilantro. Enjoy!

Nutritional Value (Amount per Serving):

Calories: 781; Protein: 17.24; Fat: 62.38; Carbs: 54.68

Mexican Quinoa Stuffed Peppers

Prep Time: 15 mins
Cook Time: 40 mins
Servings: 4

Ingredients:

- 4 bell peppers (any color), tops removed and seeds removed
- 1 cup quinoa
- 1 cup corn kernels
- 1 can black beans, drained and rinsed
- 1 cup salsa
- 1 teaspoon chili powder
- 1/2 teaspoon cumin
- 1/2 teaspoon paprika
- Salt and pepper to taste
- 1/2 cup shredded cheddar cheese (optional)
- Fresh cilantro, chopped (for garnish)

Directions:

1. Preheat the oven to 375°F. Place the bell peppers in a baking dish.
2. Rinse the quinoa thoroughly under cold water. In a medium saucepan, bring 2 cups of water to a boil. Add the quinoa and reduce the heat to low. Cover and simmer for about 15-20 minutes, or until the quinoa is cooked and the water is absorbed. Fluff with a fork and let it cool slightly.
3. In a large bowl, combine the cooked quinoa, black beans, corn kernels, salsa, chili powder, cumin, paprika, salt, and pepper. Stir well to combine.
4. Spoon the quinoa mixture into the bell peppers, filling them to the top. If desired, sprinkle shredded cheddar cheese on top of each pepper.
5. Cover the baking dish with foil and bake for 30 minutes. Then, remove the foil and bake for an additional 10 minutes, or until the peppers are tender and the cheese is melted and bubbly.
6. Remove from the oven and let the stuffed peppers cool for a few minutes. Garnish with fresh cilantro before serving. Enjoy!

Nutritional Value (Amount per Serving):

Calories: 231; Protein: 9.28; Fat: 3.57; Carbs: 43.8

Mediterranean Couscous

Prep Time: 15 mins
Cook Time: 10 mins
Servings: 6

Ingredients:

- 1 1/2 cups couscous
- 1 1/2 cups vegetable broth
- 1 cup cherry tomatoes, halved
- 1 cucumber, diced
- 1/2 red onion, diced
- 1/2 cup Kalamata olives, pitted and halved
- 1/4 cup fresh parsley, chopped
- 1/4 cup fresh mint, chopped
- 1/4 cup olive oil
- 2 tablespoons lemon juice
- 1 clove garlic, minced
- Salt and pepper to taste
- Feta cheese, crumbled (for garnish)

Directions:

1. In a medium saucepan, bring the vegetable broth to a boil. Remove from heat and stir in the couscous. Cover and let it sit for about 5 minutes, or until the couscous absorbs the liquid. Fluff with a fork and let it cool.
2. In a large bowl, combine the cooked couscous, cherry tomatoes, cucumber, red onion, Kalamata olives, parsley, and mint.
3. In a small bowl, whisk together the olive oil, lemon juice, garlic, salt, and pepper. Pour the dressing over the couscous mixture and toss to combine.
4. Adjust the seasoning if needed. Serve the Mediterranean couscous chilled or at room temperature. Sprinkle with crumbled feta cheese before serving. Enjoy!

Nutritional Value (Amount per Serving):

Calories: 714; Protein: 7.7; Fat: 70.96; Carbs: 17.44

Cajun Red Beans and Rice

Prep Time: 15 mins
Cook Time: 1 hour 30 mins
Servings: 6

Ingredients:

- 1 cup dried red kidney beans
- 1 cup long-grain white rice
- 1 onion, diced
- 1 green bell pepper, diced
- 2 celery stalks, diced
- 3 cloves garlic, minced
- 1 can diced tomatoes
- 2 bay leaves
- 2 teaspoons Cajun seasoning
- 1 teaspoon dried thyme
- 1 teaspoon dried oregano
- 1/2 teaspoon paprika
- 1/2 teaspoon cayenne pepper (optional)
- Salt and pepper to taste
- Fresh parsley, chopped (for garnish)

Directions:

1. Rinse the red kidney beans under cold water. In a large pot, add the beans and enough water to cover them by about 2 inches. Bring to a boil over high heat, then reduce the heat to low and let it simmer for about 1 hour, or until the beans are tender. Drain and set aside.
2. In a separate pot, cook the white rice according to package instructions.
3. In the same pot used for cooking the beans, heat some oil over medium heat. Add the onion, green bell pepper, and celery. Cook until the vegetables are softened, about 5 minutes.
4. Add the garlic, diced tomatoes, bay leaves, Cajun seasoning, dried thyme, dried oregano, paprika, cayenne pepper (if using), salt, and pepper to the pot. Stir well to combine.
5. Add the cooked red kidney beans to the pot and stir everything together. Bring to a simmer and let it cook for about 30 minutes, stirring occasionally.
6. Adjust the seasoning if needed. Serve the Cajun red beans over the white rice and garnish with fresh parsley. Enjoy!

Nutritional Value (Amount per Serving):

Calories: 161; Protein: 4.21; Fat: 1.77; Carbs: 32.19

Wild Rice and Mushroom Pilaf

Prep Time: 15 mins
Cook Time: 45 mins
Servings: 4

Ingredients:

- 1 cup wild rice
- 1 tablespoon olive oil
- 2 cloves garlic, minced
- 1/4 cup white wine (optional)
- 1/4 cup dried cranberries
- 1/4 cup chopped pecans
- 2 tablespoons fresh parsley, chopped
- Salt and pepper to taste
- 2 cups vegetable broth
- 1 onion, diced
- 8 ounces mushrooms, sliced

Directions:

1. Rinse the wild rice under cold water. In a medium saucepan, bring the vegetable broth to a boil. Add the wild rice and reduce the heat to low. Cover and simmer for about 45 minutes, or until the rice is tender and the liquid is absorbed. Fluff with a fork and let it cool slightly.
2. In a large skillet, heat the olive oil over medium heat. Add the onion and garlic. Cook until the onion is translucent, about 5 minutes.
3. Add the sliced mushrooms to the skillet and cook until they release their moisture and become tender, about 8 minutes.
4. If using, pour in the white wine and cook for another 2 minutes to allow the alcohol to evaporate.
5. Add the cooked wild rice, dried cranberries, chopped pecans, fresh parsley, salt, and pepper to the skillet. Stir well to combine and cook for an additional 5 minutes to heat through.
6. Adjust the seasoning if needed. Serve the wild rice and mushroom pilaf as a side dish or as a main course. Enjoy!

Nutritional Value (Amount per Serving):

Calories: 1195; Protein: 8.96; Fat: 117.55; Carbs: 39.22

Southwestern Quinoa and Black Bean

Prep Time: 15 mins
Cook Time: 20 mins
Servings: 4

Ingredients:

- 1 cup quinoa
- 1 cup corn kernels
- 1/2 red onion, diced
- 1 jalapeno pepper, seeded and minced
- 1/4 cup fresh cilantro, chopped
- 2 tablespoons lime juice
- 2 tablespoons olive oil
- 1 teaspoon chili powder
- 1/2 teaspoon cumin
- Salt and pepper to taste
- Avocado slices (for garnish)
- 1 can black beans, drained and rinsed
- 1 red bell pepper, diced

Directions:

1. Rinse the quinoa thoroughly under cold water. In a medium saucepan, bring 2 cups of water to a boil. Add the quinoa and reduce the heat to low. Cover and simmer for about 15-20 minutes, or until the quinoa is cooked and the water is absorbed. Fluff with a fork and let it cool.
2. In a large bowl, combine the cooked quinoa, black beans, corn kernels, red bell pepper, red onion, jalapeno pepper, and cilantro.
3. In a small bowl, whisk together the lime juice, olive oil, chili powder, cumin, salt, and pepper. Pour the dressing over the quinoa mixture and toss to combine.
4. Adjust the seasoning if needed. Serve the southwestern quinoa and black bean salad chilled or at room temperature. Garnish with avocado slices before serving. Enjoy!

Nutritional Value (Amount per Serving):

Calories: 346; Protein: 8.79; Fat: 17.53; Carbs: 42.49

Italian White Bean Soup

Prep Time: 15 mins
Cook Time: 30 mins
Servings: 4

Ingredients:

- 2 tablespoons olive oil
- 1 onion, diced
- 2 carrots, diced
- 2 celery stalks, diced
- 3 cloves garlic, minced
- 2 cans white beans, drained and rinsed
- 4 cups vegetable broth
- 1 can diced tomatoes
- 1 teaspoon dried basil
- 1 teaspoon dried oregano
- 1/2 teaspoon dried thyme
- Salt and pepper to taste
- Fresh parsley, chopped (for garnish)

Directions:

1. In a large pot, heat the olive oil over medium heat. Add the onion, carrots, and celery. Cook until the vegetables are softened, about 5 minutes.
2. Add the garlic to the pot and cook for another minute.
3. Add the white beans, vegetable broth, diced tomatoes (with their juices), dried basil, dried oregano, dried thyme, salt, and pepper to the pot. Stir well to combine.
4. Bring the soup to a boil, then reduce the heat to low and let it simmer for about 20 minutes to allow the flavors to meld together.
5. Adjust the seasoning if needed. Serve the Italian white bean soup hot, garnished with fresh parsley. Enjoy!

Nutritional Value (Amount per Serving):

Calories: 1986; Protein: 1.94; Fat: 225.17; Carbs: 10.56

Moroccan Chickpea Stew

Prep Time: 15 mins
Cook Time: 40 mins
Servings: 4

Ingredients:

- 2 tablespoons olive oil
- 1 onion, diced
- 2 cloves garlic, minced
- 1 teaspoon ground cumin
- 1 teaspoon ground coriander
- 1/2 teaspoon ground cinnamon
- 1/2 teaspoon paprika
- 1/4 teaspoon cayenne pepper (optional)
- 2 cans chickpeas, drained and rinsed
- 1 can diced tomatoes
- 2 cups vegetable broth
- 1 cup butternut squash, diced
- 1 cup zucchini, diced
- 1/4 cup raisins
- Salt and pepper to taste
- Fresh cilantro, chopped (for garnish)

Directions:

1. In a large pot, heat the olive oil over medium heat. Add the onion and cook until it becomes translucent, about 5 minutes.
2. Add the garlic, ground cumin, ground coriander, ground cinnamon, paprika, and cayenne pepper (if using) to the pot. Stir well to coat the onion and spices.
3. Add the chickpeas, diced tomatoes (with their juices), vegetable broth, butternut squash, zucchini, raisins, salt, and pepper to the pot. Stir everything together.
4. Bring the stew to a boil, then reduce the heat to low and let it simmer for about 30 minutes, or until the vegetables are tender and the flavors have melded together.
5. Adjust the seasoning if needed. Serve the Moroccan chickpea stew hot, garnished with fresh cilantro. Enjoy!

Nutritional Value (Amount per Serving):

Calories: 1220; Protein: 10.53; Fat: 119.29; Carbs: 39.75

Greek Lemon Rice with Chickpeas

Prep Time: 15 mins
Cook Time: 25 mins
Servings: 4

Ingredients:

- 1 cup long-grain white rice
- 2 cups vegetable broth
- 1 can chickpeas, drained and rinsed
- 1/2 cup diced tomatoes
- 1/2 cup diced cucumber
- 1/4 cup diced red onion
- 1/4 cup chopped Kalamata olives
- 2 tablespoons fresh lemon juice
- 2 tablespoons olive oil
- 1 tablespoon chopped fresh dill
- Salt and pepper to taste
- Crumbled feta cheese (for garnish)

Directions:

1. In a medium saucepan, bring the vegetable broth to a boil. Add the white rice and reduce the heat to low. Cover and simmer for about 15-20 minutes, or until the rice is cooked and the liquid is absorbed. Fluff with a fork and let it cool slightly.
2. In a large bowl, combine the cooked rice, chickpeas, diced tomatoes, diced cucumber, diced red onion, chopped Kalamata olives, fresh lemon juice, olive oil, chopped fresh dill, salt, and pepper. Stir well to combine.
3. Adjust the seasoning if needed. Serve the Greek lemon rice with chickpeas at room temperature or chilled. Sprinkle with crumbled feta cheese before serving. Enjoy!

Nutritional Value (Amount per Serving):

Calories: 1384; Protein: 14.01; Fat: 126.85; Carbs: 57.78

Chapter 3:
Salads & Vegetables

Quinoa and Chickpea Salad

Prep Time: 15 mins
Cook Time: 20 mins
Servings: 4

Ingredients:

- 1 cup quinoa
- 2 cups water
- 1 can (15 ounces) chickpeas, drained and rinsed
- 1 cucumber, diced
- 1 red bell pepper, diced
- 1/4 cup red onion, finely chopped
- 1/4 cup fresh parsley, chopped
- 1/4 cup olive oil
- 2 tablespoons lemon juice
- Salt and pepper to taste

Directions:

1. Rinse the quinoa under cold water. In a saucepan, bring the water and quinoa to a boil. Reduce heat, cover, and simmer for 15-20 minutes or until the quinoa is tender and the water is absorbed. Remove from heat and let it cool.
2. In a large bowl, combine the cooked quinoa, chickpeas, cucumber, red bell pepper, red onion, and parsley.
3. In a small bowl, whisk together the olive oil, lemon juice, salt, and pepper. Pour the dressing over the quinoa mixture and toss to combine.
4. Serve immediately or refrigerate for later use. This salad can be stored in an airtight container in the refrigerator for up to 3 days.

Nutritional Value (Amount per Serving):

Calories: 384; Protein: 11.42; Fat: 17.86; Carbs: 46.37

Greek Salad

Prep Time: 10 mins
Total Time: 15mins
Servings: 4

Ingredients:

- 2 large tomatoes, diced
- 1 cucumber, diced
- 1/2 red onion, thinly sliced
- 1/2 cup Kalamata olives, pitted
- 1/2 cup feta cheese, crumbled
- 2 tablespoons extra virgin olive oil
- 1 tablespoon red wine vinegar
- 1 teaspoon dried oregano
- Salt and pepper to taste

Directions:

1. In a large bowl, combine the tomatoes, cucumber, red onion, Kalamata olives, and feta cheese.
2. In a small bowl, whisk together the olive oil, red wine vinegar, dried oregano, salt, and pepper.
3. Pour the dressing over the salad and toss gently to coat all the Ingredients:.
4. Serve immediately or refrigerate for later use. This salad is best when served chilled.

Nutritional Value (Amount per Serving):

Calories: 125; Protein: 4.19; Fat: 9.08; Carbs: 7.8

Roasted Vegetable Salad

Prep Time: 15 mins
Cook Time: 25 mins
Servings: 4

Ingredients:

- 1 zucchini, sliced
- 1 yellow squash, sliced
- 1 red bell pepper, sliced
- 1 red onion, sliced
- 2 tablespoons olive oil
- 1 teaspoon dried thyme
- 1/2 teaspoon garlic powder
- Salt and pepper to taste
- 4 cups mixed salad greens
- 1/4 cup balsamic vinaigrette

Directions:

1. Preheat the oven to 425°F.
2. In a large bowl, toss the zucchini, yellow squash, red bell pepper, and red onion with olive oil, dried thyme, garlic powder, salt, and pepper.
3. Spread the vegetables in a single layer on a baking sheet. Roast in the preheated oven for 20-25 minutes or until the vegetables are tender and slightly caramelized.
4. In a serving bowl, arrange the mixed salad greens. Top with the roasted vegetables.
5. Drizzle the balsamic vinaigrette over the salad and toss gently to combine.
6. Serve immediately or refrigerate for later use.

Nutritional Value (Amount per Serving):

Calories: 1569; Protein: 2.81; Fat: 171.53; Carbs: 4.29

Caprese Salad

Prep Time: 10 mins
Total Time: 15mins
Servings: 4

Ingredients:

- 2 large tomatoes, sliced
- 8 ounces fresh mozzarella cheese, sliced
- 1/4 cup fresh basil leaves
- 2 tablespoons extra virgin olive oil
- 1 tablespoon balsamic glaze
- Salt and pepper to taste

Directions:

1. Arrange the tomato slices and mozzarella slices on a serving platter, alternating them.
2. Tuck the fresh basil leaves between the tomato and mozzarella slices.
3. Drizzle the extra virgin olive oil and balsamic glaze over the salad.
4. Season with salt and pepper to taste.
5. Serve immediately as an appetizer or side dish.

Nutritional Value (Amount per Serving):

Calories: 118; Protein: 18.6; Fat: 3.09; Carbs: 4.49

Asian Quinoa Salad

Prep Time: 15 mins
Cook Time: 15 mins
Servings: 4

Ingredients:

- 1 cup quinoa
- 2 cups water
- 1 cup shredded carrots
- 1 cup shredded red cabbage
- 1/2 cup chopped green onions
- 1/4 cup chopped cilantro
- 1/4 cup soy sauce
- 2 tablespoons rice vinegar
- 1 tablespoon sesame oil
- 1 tablespoon honey
- 1 teaspoon grated ginger
- 1/4 cup chopped peanuts (optional)

Directions:

1. Rinse the quinoa under cold water. In a saucepan, bring the water and quinoa to a boil. Reduce heat, cover, and simmer for 15 minutes or until the quinoa is tender and the water is absorbed. Remove from heat and let it cool.
2. In a large bowl, combine the cooked quinoa, shredded carrots, shredded red cabbage, green onions, and cilantro.
3. In a small bowl, whisk together the soy sauce, rice vinegar, sesame oil, honey, and grated ginger. Pour the dressing over the quinoa mixture and toss to combine.
4. Sprinkle with chopped peanuts if desired.
5. Serve immediately or refrigerate for later use.

Nutritional Value (Amount per Serving):

Calories: 365; Protein: 12.5; Fat: 15.14; Carbs: 46.95

Mediterranean Couscous Salad

Prep Time: 15 mins
Cook Time: 5 mins
Servings: 4

Ingredients:

- 1 cup couscous
- 1 cup boiling water
- 1 cup diced cucumber
- 1 cup cherry tomatoes, halved
- 1/2 cup sliced Kalamata olives
- 1/4 cup crumbled feta cheese
- 2 tablespoons chopped fresh parsley
- 2 tablespoons lemon juice
- 2 tablespoons extra virgin olive oil
- Salt and pepper to taste

Directions:

1. Place the couscous in a heatproof bowl. Pour the boiling water over the couscous, cover, and let it sit for 5 minutes.
2. Fluff the couscous with a fork and let it cool.
3. In a large bowl, combine the cooked couscous, cucumber, cherry tomatoes, Kalamata olives, feta cheese, and parsley.
4. In a small bowl, whisk together the lemon juice, olive oil, salt, and pepper. Pour the dressing over the couscous mixture and toss to combine.
5. Serve immediately or refrigerate for later use.

Nutritional Value (Amount per Serving):

Calories: 147; Protein: 3.94; Fat: 7.02; Carbs: 18.36

Spinach and Strawberry Salad

Prep Time: 10 mins
Total Time: 15mins
Servings: 4

Ingredients:

- 4 cups baby spinach leaves
- 1 cup sliced strawberries
- 1/4 cup sliced almonds
- 1/4 cup crumbled goat cheese
- 2 tablespoons balsamic glaze
- 2 tablespoons extra virgin olive oil
- Salt and pepper to taste

Directions:

1. In a large bowl, combine the baby spinach leaves, sliced strawberries, sliced almonds, and crumbled goat cheese.
2. Drizzle the balsamic glaze and extra virgin olive oil over the salad.
3. Season with salt and pepper to taste.
4. Toss gently to combine all the Ingredients:.
5. Serve immediately as a refreshing salad.

Nutritional Value (Amount per Serving):

Calories: 92; Protein: 4.01; Fat: 5.89; Carbs: 7.28

Mexican Black Bean Salad

Prep Time: 10 mins
Total Time: 15mins
Servings: 4

Ingredients:

- 1 can (15 ounces) black beans, drained and rinsed
- 1 cup corn kernels (fresh or canned)
- 1/2 cup diced bell pepper (any color)
- 1/2 cup diced red onion
- 1/4 cup chopped fresh cilantro
- 2 tablespoons lime juice
- 2 tablespoons extra virgin olive oil
- 1 teaspoon ground cumin
- Salt and pepper to taste
- Tortilla chips for serving

Directions:

1. In a large bowl, combine the black beans, corn kernels, bell pepper, red onion, and cilantro.
2. In a small bowl, whisk together the lime juice, olive oil, ground cumin, salt, and pepper. Pour the dressing over the bean mixture and toss to combine.
3. Serve immediately or refrigerate for later use.
4. Serve with tortilla chips for scooping.

Nutritional Value (Amount per Serving):

Calories: 73; Protein: 1.64; Fat: 3.74; Carbs: 10.09

Waldorf Salad

Prep Time: 15 mins
Total Time: 15 mins
Servings: 4

Ingredients:

- 2 cups chopped apples
- 1 cup chopped celery
- 1/2 cup chopped walnuts
- 1/2 cup seedless grapes, halved
- 1/4 cup mayonnaise
- 1/4 cup plain Greek yogurt
- 1 tablespoon lemon juice
- 1 tablespoon honey
- Salt and pepper to taste
- Lettuce leaves for serving

Directions:

1. In a large bowl, combine the chopped apples, celery, walnuts, and grapes.
2. In a small bowl, whisk together the mayonnaise, Greek yogurt, lemon juice, honey, salt, and pepper. Pour the dressing over the apple mixture and toss to combine.
3. Serve the Waldorf salad on a bed of lettuce leaves.

Nutritional Value (Amount per Serving):

Calories: 193; Protein: 3.85; Fat: 12.02; Carbs: 20.55

Roasted Beet and Goat Cheese Salad

Prep Time: 15 mins
Cook Time: 1 hour
Servings: 4

Ingredients:

- 4 medium beets, trimmed
- 2 tablespoons olive oil
- 4 cups mixed salad greens
- 1/2 cup crumbled goat cheese
- 1/4 cup chopped walnuts
- 2 tablespoons balsamic glaze
- Salt and pepper to taste

Directions:

1. Preheat the oven to 400°F.
2. Place the beets on a baking sheet and drizzle with olive oil. Wrap the beets tightly in aluminum foil.
3. Roast the beets in the preheated oven for 1 hour or until tender when pierced with a fork. Let them cool, then peel and dice.
4. In a serving bowl, arrange the mixed salad greens. Top with the roasted beets, crumbled goat cheese, and chopped walnuts.
5. Drizzle the balsamic glaze over the salad.
6. Season with salt and pepper to taste.
7. Serve immediately or refrigerate for later use.

Nutritional Value (Amount per Serving):

Calories: 1665; Protein: 7.76; Fat: 179.8; Carbs: 5.41

Cucumber and Tomato Salad

Prep Time: 10 mins
Total Time: 15 mins
Servings: 4

Ingredients:

- 2 large cucumbers, sliced
- 2 large tomatoes, diced
- 1/4 cup red onion, thinly sliced
- 2 tablespoons chopped fresh dill
- 2 tablespoons lemon juice
- 2 tablespoons extra virgin olive oil
- Salt and pepper to taste

Directions:

1. In a large bowl, combine the sliced cucumbers, diced tomatoes, red onion, and chopped fresh dill.
2. In a small bowl, whisk together the lemon juice, olive oil, salt, and pepper. Pour the dressing over the salad and toss to combine.
3. Serve immediately as a refreshing side dish.

Nutritional Value (Amount per Serving):

Calories: 63; Protein: 1.71; Fat: 3.72; Carbs: 7.7

Chapter 4:
Fish & Seafood

Lemon Garlic Grilled Shrimp Skewers

Prep Time: 15 mins
Cook Time: 6 mins
Servings: 4

Ingredients:

- 1 pound large shrimp, peeled and deveined
- 3 cloves garlic, minced
- 2 tablespoons fresh lemon juice
- 2 tablespoons olive oil
- 1 teaspoon lemon zest
- 1/2 teaspoon salt
- 1/4 teaspoon black pepper
- 4 skewers

Directions:

1. In a bowl, combine minced garlic, lemon juice, olive oil, lemon zest, salt, and black pepper. Mix well.
2. Thread the shrimp onto skewers.
3. Brush the shrimp with the lemon garlic marinade on both sides.
4. Preheat a grill or grill pan over medium-high heat.
5. Grill the shrimp skewers for about 2-3 minutes per side, or until they turn pink and opaque.
6. Remove from the grill and serve hot. Optionally, garnish with fresh lemon wedges and parsley.

Nutritional Value (Amount per Serving):

Calories: 146; Protein: 15.63; Fat: 7.93; Carbs: 2.5

Baked Salmon with Dill Sauce

Prep Time: 10 mins
Cook Time: 15 mins
Servings: 4

Ingredients:

- 4 salmon fillets (about 6 ounces each)
- 2 tablespoons olive oil
- 1 teaspoon lemon juice
- 1/2 teaspoon salt
- 1/4 teaspoon black pepper
- 1/4 cup plain Greek yogurt
- 1 tablespoon fresh dill, chopped
- 1 teaspoon Dijon mustard
- 1 teaspoon lemon zest

Directions:

1. Preheat the oven to 400°F.
2. Place the salmon fillets on a baking sheet lined with parchment paper.
3. Drizzle the salmon with olive oil and lemon juice. Season with salt and black pepper.
4. Bake the salmon in the preheated oven for about 12-15 minutes, or until it flakes easily with a fork.
5. In a small bowl, mix together Greek yogurt, fresh dill, Dijon mustard, and lemon zest to make the dill sauce.
6. Serve the baked salmon with the dill sauce on the side.

Nutritional Value (Amount per Serving):

Calories: 76; Protein: 0.87; Fat: 7.54; Carbs: 1.99

Teriyaki Glazed Grilled Tuna Steaks

Prep Time: 10 mins
Cook Time: 6 mins
Servings: 4

Ingredients:

- 4 tuna steaks (about 6 ounces each)
- 1/4 cup soy sauce
- 2 tablespoons honey
- 2 tablespoons rice vinegar
- 1 tablespoon sesame oil
- 1 clove garlic, minced
- 1 teaspoon grated ginger
- 1/4 teaspoon red pepper flakes (optional)
- 2 green onions, chopped (for garnish)

Directions:

1. In a bowl, whisk together soy sauce, honey, rice vinegar, sesame oil, minced garlic, grated ginger, and red pepper flakes (if using).
2. Place the tuna steaks in a shallow dish and pour the teriyaki marinade over them. Let them marinate for 10 minutes.
3. Preheat a grill or grill pan over high heat.
4. Grill the tuna steaks for about 2-3 minutes per side, or until they are cooked to your desired level of doneness.
5. Remove from the grill and let them rest for a few minutes.
6. Garnish with chopped green onions and serve hot.

Nutritional Value (Amount per Serving):

Calories: 121; Protein: 1.57; Fat: 6.46; Carbs: 15.07

Cajun Shrimp and Sausage Skillet

Prep Time: 10 mins
Cook Time: 15 mins
Servings: 4

Ingredients:

- 1 pound large shrimp, peeled and deveined
- 8 ounces smoked sausage, sliced
- 1 red bell pepper, sliced
- 1 green bell pepper, sliced
- 1 yellow onion, sliced
- 2 cloves garlic, minced
- 2 tablespoons olive oil
- 1 tablespoon Cajun seasoning
- 1/2 teaspoon paprika
- 1/4 teaspoon cayenne pepper (optional)
- Salt and black pepper to taste
- 2 tablespoons fresh parsley, chopped (for garnish)

Directions:

1. Heat olive oil in a large skillet over medium heat.
2. Add sliced sausage to the skillet and cook until browned, about 3-4 minutes.
3. Add sliced bell peppers, onion, and minced garlic to the skillet. Sauté until the vegetables are tender, about 5 minutes.
4. In a small bowl, mix together Cajun seasoning, paprika, cayenne pepper (if using), salt, and black pepper.
5. Add the shrimp to the skillet and sprinkle the Cajun seasoning mixture over the shrimp and vegetables. Stir well to coat everything evenly.
6. Cook for another 3-4 minutes, or until the shrimp are pink and cooked through.
7. Garnish with fresh parsley and serve hot.

Nutritional Value (Amount per Serving):

Calories: 310; Protein: 26.91; Fat: 18.37; Carbs: 11.83

Grilled Halibut with Mango Salsa

Prep Time: 15 mins
Cook Time: 8 mins
Servings: 4

Ingredients:

- 4 halibut fillets (about 6 ounces each)
- 2 tablespoons olive oil
- 1 teaspoon lime juice
- 1/2 teaspoon ground cumin
- 1/2 teaspoon chili powder
- 1/4 teaspoon salt
- 1/4 teaspoon black pepper
- 1 ripe mango, peeled and diced
- 1/2 red bell pepper, diced
- 1/4 cup red onion, diced
- 1 jalapeño pepper, seeded and minced
- 2 tablespoons fresh cilantro, chopped
- 1 tablespoon lime juice

Directions:

1. Preheat a grill or grill pan over medium-high heat.
2. In a small bowl, whisk together olive oil, lime juice, ground cumin, chili powder, salt, and black pepper.
3. Brush the halibut fillets with the olive oil mixture on both sides.
4. Grill the halibut fillets for about 4 minutes per side, or until they are cooked through and flake easily with a fork.
5. In another bowl, combine diced mango, red bell pepper, red onion, minced jalapeño pepper, chopped cilantro, and lime juice to make the mango salsa.
6. Serve the grilled halibut with the mango salsa on top.

Nutritional Value (Amount per Serving):

Calories: 320; Protein: 20.11; Fat: 22.23; Carbs: 10.73

Lemon Herb Baked Cod

Prep Time: 10 mins
Cook Time: 15 mins
Servings: 4

Ingredients:

- 4 cod fillets (about 6 ounces each)
- 2 tablespoons olive oil
- 1 tablespoon lemon juice
- 1 teaspoon lemon zest
- 2 cloves garlic, minced
- 1 tablespoon chopped fresh parsley
- 1 tablespoon chopped fresh dill
- 1/2 teaspoon salt
- 1/4 teaspoon black pepper
- Lemon slices (for garnish)

Directions:

1. Preheat the oven to 400°F.
2. Place the cod fillets on a baking sheet lined with parchment paper.
3. In a small bowl, whisk together olive oil, lemon juice, lemon zest, minced garlic, chopped parsley, chopped dill, salt, and black pepper.
4. Brush the cod fillets with the lemon herb mixture on both sides.
5. Bake the cod in the preheated oven for about 12-15 minutes, or until it flakes easily with a fork.
6. Garnish with lemon slices and serve hot.

Nutritional Value (Amount per Serving):

Calories: 318; Protein: 20.02; Fat: 22.35; Carbs: 10.41

Coconut Curry Shrimp Stir-Fry

Prep Time: 10 mins
Cook Time: 10 mins
Servings: 4

Ingredients:

- 1 pound large shrimp, peeled and deveined
- 1 red bell pepper, sliced
- 1 cup snap peas
- 1 cup sliced mushrooms
- 1 can (15 ounces) coconut milk
- 2 tablespoons red curry paste
- 1 tablespoon fish sauce
- 1 tablespoon lime juice
- 1 tablespoon brown sugar
- 1/4 cup fresh basil leaves, torn
- 1 tablespoon coconut oil
- 1 yellow bell pepper, sliced

Directions:

1. Heat coconut oil in a large skillet or wok over medium-high heat.
2. Add the shrimp to the skillet and cook until pink and cooked through, about 2-3 minutes. Remove the shrimp from the skillet and set aside.
3. In the same skillet, add sliced bell peppers, snap peas, and mushrooms. Stir-fry for about 3-4 minutes, or until the vegetables are crisp-tender.
4. In a small bowl, whisk together coconut milk, red curry paste, fish sauce, lime juice, and brown sugar.
5. Pour the coconut curry sauce into the skillet with the vegetables. Cook for another 2 minutes, stirring occasionally.
6. Add the cooked shrimp back to the skillet and toss to coat everything in the sauce.
7. Remove from heat and garnish with torn fresh basil leaves.
8. Serve the coconut curry shrimp stir-fry over steamed rice or noodles.

Nutritional Value (Amount per Serving):

Calories: 148; Protein: 16.79; Fat: 4.81; Carbs: 9.46

Honey Mustard Glazed Salmon

Prep Time: 10 mins
Cook Time: 12 mins
Servings: 4

Ingredients:

- 4 salmon fillets (about 6 ounces each)
- 2 tablespoons Dijon mustard
- 2 tablespoons honey
- 1 tablespoon whole grain mustard
- 1 tablespoon lemon juice
- 1/2 teaspoon garlic powder
- 1/2 teaspoon onion powder
- 1/4 teaspoon salt
- 1/4 teaspoon black pepper
- 1 tablespoon chopped fresh parsley (for garnish)

Directions:

1. Preheat the oven to 400°F.
2. Place the salmon fillets on a baking sheet lined with parchment paper.
3. In a small bowl, whisk together Dijon mustard, honey, whole grain mustard, lemon juice, garlic powder, onion powder, salt, and black pepper.
4. Brush the honey mustard glaze over the top of each salmon fillet.
5. Bake the salmon in the preheated oven for about 10-12 minutes, or until it flakes easily with a fork.
6. Garnish with chopped fresh parsley and serve hot.

Nutritional Value (Amount per Serving):

Calories: 47; Protein: 0.63; Fat: 0.36; Carbs: 11.53

Shrimp Scampi with Linguine

Prep Time: 10 mins
Cook Time: 15 mins
Servings: 4

Ingredients:

- 8 ounces linguine
- 4 tablespoons unsalted butter
- 4 cloves garlic, minced
- 1/4 teaspoon red pepper flakes
- 1/4 cup white wine
- 1 tablespoon lemon juice
- 1/4 cup chopped fresh parsley
- Salt and black pepper to taste
- Grated Parmesan cheese (optional, for serving)
- 1 pound large shrimp, peeled and deveined

Directions:

1. Cook the linguine according to the package instructions until al dente. Drain and set aside.
2. In a large skillet, melt the butter over medium heat.
3. Add minced garlic and red pepper flakes to the skillet. Sauté for about 1 minute, until the garlic becomes fragrant.
4. Add the shrimp to the skillet and cook for 2-3 minutes on each side, until they turn pink and opaque.
5. Pour in the white wine and lemon juice. Cook for another minute to let the flavors meld.
6. Add the cooked linguine to the skillet and toss to coat the pasta in the garlic butter sauce.
7. Stir in chopped fresh parsley and season with salt and black pepper.
8. Serve the shrimp scampi with linguine hot, optionally garnished with grated Parmesan cheese.

Nutritional Value (Amount per Serving):

Calories: 162; Protein: 16.51; Fat: 8.94; Carbs: 3.7

Blackened Catfish with Cilantro Lime

Prep Time: 10 mins
Cook Time: 8 mins
Servings: 4

Ingredients:

- 4 catfish fillets (about 6 ounces each)
- 1 teaspoon dried thyme
- 1 teaspoon dried oregano
- 1/2 teaspoon garlic powder
- 1/2 teaspoon onion powder
- 1/2 teaspoon cayenne pepper
- 1/2 teaspoon salt
- 1/4 teaspoon black pepper
- 2 tablespoons olive oil
- 1/4 cup mayonnaise
- 1 tablespoon lime juice
- 2 tablespoons chopped fresh cilantro

- 2 teaspoons paprika

Directions:

1. In a small bowl, combine paprika, dried thyme, dried oregano, garlic powder, onion powder, cayenne pepper, salt, and black pepper to make the blackened seasoning.
2. Pat the catfish fillets dry with paper towels and sprinkle both sides with the blackened seasoning.
3. Heat olive oil in a large skillet over medium-high heat.
4. Add the catfish fillets to the skillet and cook for about 3-4 minutes per side, or until they are blackened and cooked through.
5. In a separate bowl, whisk together mayonnaise, lime juice, and chopped cilantro to make the cilantro lime sauce.
6. Serve the blackened catfish fillets with a drizzle of cilantro lime sauce.

Nutritional Value (Amount per Serving):

Calories: 268; Protein: 27.3; Fat: 16.22; Carbs: 2.4

Grilled Swordfish with Herb Butter

Prep Time: 10 mins
Cook Time: 8 mins
Servings: 4

Ingredients:

- 4 swordfish steaks (about 6 ounces each)
- 2 tablespoons olive oil
- 1 teaspoon lemon zest
- 1 teaspoon chopped fresh thyme
- 1 teaspoon chopped fresh rosemary
- 1/2 teaspoon salt
- 1/4 teaspoon black pepper
- 4 tablespoons unsalted butter, softened
- 1 tablespoon chopped fresh parsley

Directions:

1. Preheat a grill or grill pan over medium-high heat.
2. In a small bowl, combine olive oil, lemon zest, chopped thyme, chopped rosemary, salt, and black pepper to make the herb marinade.
3. Brush the swordfish steaks with the herb marinade on both sides.
4. Grill the swordfish steaks for about 3-4 minutes per side, or until they are cooked through and have grill marks.
5. In another bowl, mix together softened butter and chopped parsley to make the herb butter.
6. Place a dollop of herb butter on top of each grilled swordfish steak. Let it melt slightly before serving.

Nutritional Value (Amount per Serving):

Calories: 131; Protein: 0.53; Fat: 14.49; Carbs: 0.35

Chapter 5: Meat

Coconut Curry Chicken

Prep Time: 15 mins
Cook Time: 30 mins
Servings: 4

Ingredients:

- 5 pounds boneless, skinless chicken breasts, cut into bite-sized pieces
- 1 tablespoon vegetable oil
- 1 onion, chopped
- 3 cloves garlic, minced
- 1 tablespoon grated fresh ginger
- 2 tablespoons curry powder
- 1 can (14 ounces) coconut milk
- 1 cup chicken broth
- 1 red bell pepper, sliced
- 1 cup frozen peas
- 1 tablespoon lime juice
- Salt and pepper to taste
- Cooked rice for serving
- Fresh cilantro for garnish (optional)

Directions:

1. Heat the vegetable oil in a large skillet or pot over medium heat.
2. Add the chopped onion, minced garlic, and grated ginger to the skillet. Cook for 2-3 minutes, until the onion is translucent and fragrant.
3. Add the curry powder to the skillet and cook for an additional 1 minute, stirring constantly.
4. Add the chicken pieces to the skillet and cook until browned on all sides, about 5 minutes.
5. Pour in the coconut milk and chicken broth. Stir to combine.
6. Bring the mixture to a simmer and let it cook for 15 minutes, or until the chicken is cooked through and tender.
7. Add the sliced red bell pepper and frozen peas to the skillet. Cook for an additional 5 minutes, until the vegetables are heated through.
8. Stir in the lime juice and season with salt and pepper to taste.
9. Serve the coconut curry chicken over cooked rice. Garnish with fresh cilantro if desired.

Nutritional Value (Amount per Serving):

Calories: 485; Protein: 31.51; Fat: 18.08; Carbs: 48.9

Savory Beef Stir-Fry

Prep Time: 20 mins
Cook Time: 10 mins
Servings: 4

Ingredients:

- 1 pound beef sirloin, thinly sliced
- 2 tablespoons soy sauce
- 1 tablespoon cornstarch
- 1 tablespoon vegetable oil
- 1 bell pepper, thinly sliced
- 1 onion, thinly sliced
- 2 cloves garlic, minced
- 1 teaspoon ginger, grated

Directions:

1. In a bowl, combine soy sauce and cornstarch. Add beef slices and toss to coat evenly.
2. Heat vegetable oil in a large skillet or wok over high heat. Add beef and stir-fry for 2-3 minutes until browned. Remove beef from the skillet and set aside.
3. In the same skillet, add bell pepper, onion, garlic, and ginger. Stir-fry for 2-3 minutes until vegetables are crisp-tender.
4. Return beef to the skillet and cook for an additional 2 minutes, stirring constantly.
5. Serve hot and enjoy!

Nutritional Value (Amount per Serving):

Calories: 283; Protein: 24.38; Fat: 17.5; Carbs: 5.67

Herb-Roasted Lamb Chops

Prep Time: 10 mins
Cook Time: 20 mins
Servings: 2

Ingredients:

- 4 lamb chops
- 2 tablespoons olive oil
- 2 cloves garlic, minced
- 1 tablespoon fresh rosemary, chopped
- 1 tablespoon fresh thyme, chopped
- Salt and pepper to taste

Directions:

1. Preheat the oven to 400°F.
2. In a small bowl, combine olive oil, minced garlic, rosemary, thyme, salt, and pepper.
3. Rub the herb mixture over both sides of the lamb chops.
4. Heat a skillet over medium-high heat. Sear the lamb chops for 2 minutes on each side until browned.
5. Transfer the lamb chops to a baking sheet and roast in the preheated oven for about 12-15 minutes for medium-rare doneness.
6. Remove from the oven and let the lamb chops rest for a few minutes before serving.

Nutritional Value (Amount per Serving):

Calories: 135; Protein: 0.74; Fat: 13.63; Carbs: 3.59

Crispy Duck with Orange Glaze

Prep Time: 15 mins
Cook Time: 1 hour 30 mins
Servings: 4

Ingredients:

- 1 whole duck (about 4 pounds)
- Salt and pepper to taste
- 1 orange, zest and juice
- 2 tablespoons honey
- 2 tablespoons soy sauce
- 1 tablespoon cornstarch
- 1 tablespoon water

Directions:

1. Preheat the oven to 375°F.
2. Pat the duck dry with paper towels and season with salt and pepper.
3. Place the duck on a rack in a roasting pan and roast for about 1 hour and 15 minutes until the skin is crispy and golden brown.
4. In a small saucepan, combine orange zest, orange juice, honey, and soy sauce. Bring to a simmer over medium heat.
5. In a separate bowl, mix cornstarch and water to make a slurry. Add the slurry to the simmering sauce and cook until thickened, stirring constantly.
6. Remove the duck from the oven and brush with the orange glaze. Return to the oven for an additional 10-15 minutes.
7. Let the duck rest for a few minutes before carving. Serve with remaining orange glaze.

Nutritional Value (Amount per Serving):

Calories: 352; Protein: 24.35; Fat: 21.99; Carbs: 13.52

Spicy Beef Tacos

Prep Time: 15 mins
Cook Time: 15 mins
Servings: 4

Ingredients:

- 1 pound ground beef
- 1 tablespoon vegetable oil
- 1 onion, chopped
- 2 cloves garlic, minced
- 1 tablespoon chili powder
- 1 teaspoon cumin
- 1 teaspoon paprika
- 1/2 teaspoon cayenne pepper (optional)
- Salt and pepper to taste
- 8 small flour tortillas
- Toppings: shredded lettuce, diced tomatoes, shredded cheese, salsa, sour cream

Directions:

1. Heat vegetable oil in a skillet over medium heat. Add onion and garlic, and cook until softened.
2. Add ground beef to the skillet and cook until browned, breaking it up with a spoon.
3. Stir in chili powder, cumin, paprika, cayenne pepper (if using), salt, and pepper. Cook for an additional 2-3 minutes.
4. Warm the flour tortillas in a separate skillet or in the oven.
5. Fill each tortilla with the beef mixture and top with desired toppings.
6. Serve hot and enjoy!

Nutritional Value (Amount per Serving):

Calories: 578; Protein: 38.92; Fat: 22.11; Carbs: 54.21

Grilled Lamb Kebabs

Prep Time: 20 mins
Cook Time: 10 mins
Servings: 4

Ingredients:

- 1 pound lamb leg or shoulder, cut into 1-inch cubes
- 2 tablespoons olive oil
- 2 cloves garlic, minced
- 1 teaspoon ground cumin
- 1 teaspoon ground coriander
- 1 teaspoon paprika
- Salt and pepper to taste
- Skewers, soaked in water if wooden

Directions:

1. In a bowl, combine olive oil, minced garlic, cumin, coriander, paprika, salt, and pepper.
2. Add the lamb cubes to the marinade and toss to coat evenly. Let marinate for at least 15 minutes or up to overnight in the refrigerator.
3. Preheat the grill to medium-high heat.
4. Thread the marinated lamb cubes onto skewers.
5. Grill the kebabs for about 8-10 minutes, turning occasionally, until the lamb is cooked to your desired doneness.
6. Remove from the grill and let the kebabs rest for a few minutes before serving.

Nutritional Value (Amount per Serving):

Calories: 222; Protein: 23.41; Fat: 12.96; Carbs: 2.11

Duck Confit with Roasted Potatoes

Prep Time: 15 mins
Cook Time: 2 hours 30 mins
Servings: 4

Ingredients:

- 4 duck legs
- Salt and pepper to taste
- 4 sprigs fresh thyme
- 4 cloves garlic, smashed
- 2 pounds potatoes, cut into wedges
- 2 tablespoons olive oil
- Salt and pepper to taste

Directions:

1. Preheat the oven to 300°F.
2. Season the duck legs generously with salt and pepper. Place them in a single layer in a baking dish.
3. Add thyme sprigs and smashed garlic cloves to the baking dish.
4. Cover the dish with foil and roast in the preheated oven for about 2 hours until the duck is tender.
5. Increase the oven temperature to 425°F.
6. In a separate baking dish, toss the potato wedges with olive oil, salt, and pepper.
7. Roast the potatoes in the oven for about 30 minutes until golden brown and crispy.
8. Serve the duck confit with the roasted potatoes.

Nutritional Value (Amount per Serving):

Calories: 447; Protein: 29.83; Fat: 17.5; Carbs: 42.74

Korean Beef Bulgogi

Prep Time: 15 mins
Marinating Time: 1 hour
Cook Time: 10 mins
Servings: 4

Ingredients:

- 1 pound beef sirloin, thinly sliced
- ¼ cup soy sauce
- 2 tablespoons brown sugar
- 2 tablespoons sesame oil
- 4 cloves garlic, minced
- 1 tablespoon grated fresh ginger
- 2 green onions, thinly sliced
- 1 tablespoon sesame seeds

Directions:

1. In a bowl, combine soy sauce, brown sugar, sesame oil, minced garlic, grated ginger, sliced green onions, and sesame seeds.
2. Add the beef slices to the marinade and toss to coat evenly. Let marinate for at least 1 hour in the refrigerator.
3. Heat a skillet or grill pan over high heat.
4. Cook the marinated beef in batches for about 2-3 minutes per side until browned and cooked through.
5. Serve the bulgogi with steamed rice and enjoy!

Nutritional Value (Amount per Serving):

Calories: 355; Protein: 25.21; Fat: 23.56; Carbs: 9.45

Lamb Curry

Prep Time: 20 mins
Cook Time: 1 hour 30 mins
Servings: 6

Ingredients:

- 2 pounds lamb shoulder, cut into cubes
- 2 tablespoons vegetable oil
- 2 onions, chopped
- 4 cloves garlic, minced
- 1 tablespoon grated fresh ginger
- 2 tablespoons curry powder
- 1 teaspoon ground cumin
- 1 teaspoon ground coriander
- 1 teaspoon ground turmeric
- 1 can (14 ounces) diced tomatoes
- 1 cup coconut milk
- Salt and pepper to taste
- Chopped fresh cilantro for garnish

Directions:

1. Heat vegetable oil in a large pot or Dutch oven over medium heat. Add onions, garlic, and ginger, and cook until softened.
2. Add lamb cubes to the pot and brown on all sides.
3. Stir in curry powder, cumin, coriander, and turmeric. Cook for an additional minute.
4. Add diced tomatoes with their juices and coconut milk to the pot. Season with salt and pepper.
5. Bring the mixture to a simmer, then reduce the heat to low. Cover and simmer for about 1 hour and 30 minutes until the lamb is tender.
6. Serve the lamb curry over steamed rice and garnish with chopped cilantro.

Nutritional Value (Amount per Serving):

Calories: 389; Protein: 39.16; Fat: 21.84; Carbs: 9.68

Crispy Peking Duck Pancakes

Prep Time: 20 mins
Cook Time: 2 hours
Servings: 4

Ingredients:

- 1 whole duck (about 4-5 pounds)
- 2 tablespoons honey
- 2 tablespoons soy sauce
- 1 tablespoon hoisin sauce
- 1 tablespoon rice vinegar
- 1 teaspoon Chinese five-spice powder
- 1 cucumber, julienned
- 8-12 small flour pancakes

Directions:

1. Preheat the oven to 300°F.
2. Place the duck on a rack in a roasting pan and roast for about 2 hours until the skin is crispy and golden brown.
3. In a small bowl, whisk together honey, soy sauce, hoisin sauce, rice vinegar, and Chinese five-spice powder.
4. Remove the duck from the oven and brush the skin with the honey glaze. Return to the oven for an additional 10 minutes.
5. Let the duck rest for a few minutes before carving.
6. Serve the crispy duck with julienned cucumber and small flour pancakes. To assemble, spread hoisin sauce on a pancake, add slices of duck and cucumber, and roll it up.

Nutritional Value (Amount per Serving):

Calories: 595; Protein: 29.94; Fat: 29.19; Carbs: 52.29

Beef and Broccoli Stir-Fry

Prep Time: 15 mins
Cook Time: 10 mins
Servings: 4

Ingredients:

- 1 pound beef sirloin, thinly sliced
- 2 tablespoons soy sauce
- 1 tablespoon oyster sauce
- 1 tablespoon cornstarch
- 1 tablespoon vegetable oil
- 2 cloves garlic, minced
- 1 teaspoon grated fresh ginger
- 4 cups broccoli florets
- Salt and pepper to taste

Directions:

1. In a bowl, combine soy sauce, oyster sauce, and cornstarch. Add beef slices and toss to coat evenly.
2. Heat vegetable oil in a large skillet or wok over high heat. Add minced garlic and grated ginger, and cook for about 30 seconds until fragrant.
3. Add beef to the skillet and stir-fry for 2-3 minutes until browned. Remove beef from the skillet and set aside.
4. In the same skillet, add broccoli florets and stir-fry for 2-3 minutes until crisp-tender.
5. Return beef to the skillet and cook for an additional 2 minutes, stirring constantly.
6. Season with salt and pepper to taste.
7. Serve hot over steamed rice or noodles.

Nutritional Value (Amount per Serving):

Calories: 293; Protein: 25.68; Fat: 17.71; Carbs: 7.09

Duck Breast with Raspberry Sauce

Prep Time: 10 mins
Cook Time: 20 mins
Servings: 2

Ingredients:

- 2 duck breasts
- Salt and pepper to taste
- 1 cup fresh or frozen raspberries
- 2 tablespoons balsamic vinegar
- 2 tablespoons honey
- 1 tablespoon butter

Directions:

1. Score the skin of the duck breasts in a crisscross pattern and season with salt and pepper.
2. Heat a skillet over medium heat. Place the duck breasts skin-side down and cook for about 8-10 minutes until the skin is crispy and browned.
3. Flip the duck breasts and cook for an additional 4-5 minutes for medium-rare doneness. Adjust the cooking time based on your preference.
4. Remove the duck breasts from the skillet and let them rest for a few minutes.
5. In the same skillet, add raspberries, balsamic vinegar, and honey. Cook over medium heat until the raspberries break down and the sauce thickens, about 5 minutes.
6. Stir in butter until melted and well combined.
7. Slice the duck breasts and serve with the raspberry sauce drizzled on top.

Nutritional Value (Amount per Serving):

Calories: 471; Protein: 34.48; Fat: 13.06; Carbs: 54.86

Chapter 6: Poultry

Lemon Herb Roasted Chicken

Prep Time: 15 mins
Cook Time: 1 hour 30 mins
Servings: 4

Ingredients:

- 1 whole chicken (about 4 pounds)
- 2 lemons, sliced
- 4 cloves garlic, minced
- 2 tablespoons fresh rosemary, chopped
- 2 tablespoons fresh thyme, chopped
- 2 tablespoons olive oil
- Salt and pepper to taste

Directions:

1. Preheat the oven to 375°F.
2. Rinse the chicken and pat it dry with paper towels. Place it on a roasting rack in a roasting pan.
3. In a small bowl, combine the minced garlic, chopped rosemary, chopped thyme, olive oil, salt, and pepper.
4. Rub the herb mixture all over the chicken, both on the outside and inside the cavity.
5. Stuff the cavity of the chicken with the sliced lemons.
6. Place the roasting pan in the preheated oven and roast the chicken for about 1 hour and 30 minutes, or until the internal temperature reaches 165°F when measured with a meat thermometer inserted into the thickest part of the thigh.
7. Remove the chicken from the oven and let it rest for 10 minutes before carving. Serve hot.

Nutritional Value (Amount per Serving):

Calories: 341; Protein: 49.08; Fat: 13.35; Carbs: 4.18

Teriyaki Chicken Stir-Fry

Prep Time: 15 mins
Cook Time: 15 mins
Servings: 4

Ingredients:

- 1 pound boneless, skinless chicken breasts, thinly sliced
- 1/4 cup soy sauce
- 2 tablespoons honey
- 2 tablespoons rice vinegar
- 1 tablespoon cornstarch
- 1 tablespoon vegetable oil
- 1 red bell pepper, sliced
- 1 green bell pepper, sliced
- 1 small onion, sliced
- 2 cloves garlic, minced
- 1 teaspoon grated fresh ginger
- Sesame seeds for garnish (optional)
- Cooked rice for serving

Directions:

1. In a small bowl, whisk together the soy sauce, honey, rice vinegar, and cornstarch. Set aside.
2. Heat the vegetable oil in a large skillet or wok over medium-high heat.
3. Add the sliced chicken to the skillet and cook until browned and cooked through, about 5 minutes. Remove the chicken from the skillet and set aside.
4. In the same skillet, add the sliced bell peppers and onion. Cook for 3-4 minutes, until the vegetables are crisp-tender.
5. Add the minced garlic and grated ginger to the skillet and cook for an additional 1 minute.
6. Return the cooked chicken to the skillet and pour the teriyaki sauce over the chicken and vegetables. Stir to coat everything evenly.
7. Cook for 1-2 minutes, until the sauce thickens.
8. Remove from heat and garnish with sesame seeds if desired. Serve over cooked rice.

Nutritional Value (Amount per Serving):

Calories: 337; Protein: 12.44; Fat: 12.91; Carbs: 43.16

BBQ Pulled Chicken Sandwiches

Prep Time: 15 mins
Cook Time: 4 hours
Servings: 6

Ingredients:

- 2 pounds boneless, skinless chicken breasts
- 1 cup barbecue sauce
- 1/4 cup apple cider vinegar
- 1/4 cup brown sugar
- 1 tablespoon Worcestershire sauce
- 1 tablespoon Dijon mustard
- 1 teaspoon smoked paprika
- 1/2 teaspoon garlic powder
- 1/2 teaspoon onion powder
- Salt and pepper to taste
- 6 hamburger buns

Directions:

1. Place the chicken breasts in a slow cooker.
2. In a medium bowl, whisk together the barbecue sauce, apple cider vinegar, brown sugar, Worcestershire sauce, Dijon mustard, smoked paprika, garlic powder, onion powder, salt, and pepper.
3. Pour the sauce mixture over the chicken in the slow cooker.
4. Cover the slow cooker and cook on low heat for 4 hours, or until the chicken is tender and easily shreds with a fork.
5. Remove the chicken from the slow cooker and shred it using two forks.
6. Return the shredded chicken to the slow cooker and stir it into the sauce.
7. Toast the hamburger buns if desired. Spoon the pulled chicken onto the buns and serve hot.

Nutritional Value (Amount per Serving):

Calories: 373; Protein: 14.77; Fat: 9.06; Carbs: 57.24

Baked Parmesan Crusted Chicken

Prep Time: 15 mins
Cook Time: 25 mins
Servings: 4

Ingredients:

- 4 boneless, skinless chicken breasts
- 1/2 cup grated Parmesan cheese
- 1/2 cup breadcrumbs
- 1 teaspoon dried oregano
- 1 teaspoon dried basil
- 1/2 teaspoon garlic powder
- 1/2 teaspoon onion powder
- Salt and pepper to taste
- 2 tablespoons melted butter

Directions:

1. Preheat the oven to 400°F. Grease a baking sheet or line it with parchment paper.
2. In a shallow dish, combine the grated Parmesan cheese, breadcrumbs, dried oregano, dried basil, garlic powder, onion powder, salt, and pepper.
3. Dip each chicken breast into the melted butter, then coat it with the Parmesan mixture, pressing the mixture onto the chicken to adhere.
4. Place the coated chicken breasts on the prepared baking sheet.
5. Bake in the preheated oven for 20-25 minutes, or until the chicken is cooked through and the coating is golden brown.
6. Remove from the oven and let the chicken rest for a few minutes before serving. Serve hot.

Nutritional Value (Amount per Serving):

Calories: 111; Protein: 4; Fat: 9.29; Carbs: 3.59

Lemon Garlic Herb Grilled Chicken

Prep Time: 15 mins
Cook Time: 15 mins
Servings: 4

Ingredients:

- 4 boneless, skinless chicken breasts
- 1/4 cup olive oil
- 2 tablespoons fresh lemon juice
- 4 cloves garlic, minced
- 1 tablespoon chopped fresh parsley
- 1 tablespoon chopped fresh rosemary
- 1 tablespoon chopped fresh thyme
- Salt and pepper to taste

Directions:

1. Preheat the grill to medium-high heat.
2. In a small bowl, whisk together the olive oil, lemon juice, minced garlic, chopped parsley, chopped rosemary, chopped thyme, salt, and pepper.
3. Place the chicken breasts in a shallow dish and pour the marinade over them, turning to coat both sides.
4. Let the chicken marinate for at least 15 minutes, or up to 1 hour for more flavor.
5. Remove the chicken from the marinade and discard the remaining marinade.
6. Place the chicken breasts on the preheated grill and cook for 6-7 minutes per side, or until the internal temperature reaches 165°F when measured with a meat thermometer inserted into the thickest part of the chicken.
7. Remove the chicken from the grill and let it rest for a few minutes before serving. Serve hot.

Nutritional Value (Amount per Serving):

Calories: 131; Protein: 0.52; Fat: 13.6; Carbs: 2.88

Greek Lemon Chicken and Rice

Prep Time: 15 mins
Cook Time: 1 hour
Servings: 6

Ingredients:

- 3 pounds chicken pieces (legs, thighs, or a combination)
- 1 cup long-grain white rice
- 1/4 cup fresh lemon juice
- 1 teaspoon dried oregano
- 1 teaspoon dried rosemary
- 1/2 teaspoon black pepper
- 2 cups chicken broth
- 1 lemon, sliced
- Fresh parsley for garnish
- 1/4 cup olive oil
- 4 cloves garlic, minced
- 1 teaspoon dried thyme
- 1 teaspoon salt

Directions:

1. Preheat the oven to 375°F.
2. In a large bowl, combine the olive oil, lemon juice, minced garlic, dried oregano, dried thyme, dried rosemary, salt, and black pepper.
3. Add the chicken pieces to the bowl and toss to coat them with the marinade.
4. In a 9x13-inch baking dish, spread the rice evenly on the bottom.
5. Place the marinated chicken pieces on top of the rice.
6. Pour the chicken broth over the rice and chicken.
7. Arrange the lemon slices on top of the chicken.
8. Cover the baking dish with foil and bake in the preheated oven for 45 minutes.
9. Remove the foil and continue baking for an additional 15 minutes, or until the chicken is cooked through and the rice is tender.
10. Remove from the oven and let it rest for a few minutes before serving. Garnish with fresh parsley.

Nutritional Value (Amount per Serving):

Calories: 599; Protein: 63.18; Fat: 24.39; Carbs: 27.51

Honey Mustard Baked Chicken Thighs

Prep Time: 15 mins
Cook Time: 35 mins
Servings: 4

Ingredients:

- 8 bone-in, skin-on chicken thighs
- 1/4 cup Dijon mustard
- 1/4 cup honey
- 2 tablespoons olive oil
- 2 cloves garlic, minced
- 1 teaspoon dried thyme
- 1/2 teaspoon paprika
- Salt and pepper to taste

Directions:

1. Preheat the oven to 400°F. Grease a baking dish.
2. In a small bowl, whisk together the Dijon mustard, honey, olive oil, minced garlic, dried thyme, paprika, salt, and pepper.
3. Place the chicken thighs in the prepared baking dish.
4. Pour the honey mustard mixture over the chicken thighs, spreading it evenly to coat them.
5. Bake in the preheated oven for 30-35 minutes, or until the chicken is cooked through and the skin is crispy and golden brown.
6. Remove from the oven and let the chicken rest for a few minutes before serving. Serve hot.

Nutritional Value (Amount per Serving):

Calories: 141; Protein: 1.02; Fat: 7.34; Carbs: 20.15

Buffalo Chicken Lettuce Wraps

Prep Time: 15 mins
Cook Time: 15 mins
Servings: 4

Ingredients:

- 1 pound boneless, skinless chicken breasts, cooked and shredded
- 1/2 cup buffalo sauce
- 1/4 cup ranch dressing
- 8 large lettuce leaves (such as iceberg or butter lettuce)
- 1/2 cup diced tomatoes
- 1/4 cup diced red onion
- 1/4 cup crumbled blue cheese (optional)
- Fresh cilantro for garnish (optional)

Directions:

1. In a medium bowl, combine the shredded chicken with the buffalo sauce, tossing to coat the chicken evenly.
2. In a small bowl, mix the ranch dressing with the blue cheese (if using).
3. Place a spoonful of the buffalo chicken mixture onto each lettuce leaf.
4. Top the chicken with diced tomatoes and red onion.
5. Drizzle the ranch dressing mixture over the toppings.
6. Garnish with fresh cilantro if desired.
7. Roll up the lettuce leaves to form wraps and serve immediately.

Nutritional Value (Amount per Serving):

Calories: 306; Protein: 13.26; Fat: 15.66; Carbs: 28.33

Oven-Baked Chicken Fajitas

Prep Time: 15 mins
Cook Time: 25 mins
Servings: 4

Ingredients:

- 1 pound boneless, skinless chicken breasts, thinly sliced
- 1 red bell pepper, sliced
- 1 green bell pepper, sliced
- 1 yellow bell pepper, sliced
- 1 onion, sliced
- 2 tablespoons olive oil
- 1 tablespoon chili powder
- 1 teaspoon ground cumin
- 1 teaspoon paprika
- 1/2 teaspoon garlic powder
- 1/2 teaspoon onion powder
- Salt and pepper to taste
- Flour tortillas
- Toppings: shredded cheese, sour cream, guacamole, salsa, etc.

Directions:

1. Preheat the oven to 400°F. Grease a baking sheet.
2. In a small bowl, combine the chili powder, ground cumin, paprika, garlic powder, onion powder, salt, and pepper.
3. In a large bowl, toss the chicken, bell peppers, and onion with the olive oil.
4. Sprinkle the spice mixture over the chicken and vegetables, tossing to coat them evenly.
5. Spread the chicken and vegetables in a single layer on the prepared baking sheet.
6. Bake in the preheated oven for 20-25 minutes, or until the chicken is cooked through and the vegetables are tender.
7. Warm the flour tortillas according to package instructions.
8. Serve the oven-baked chicken fajitas with warm tortillas and your choice of toppings.

Nutritional Value (Amount per Serving):

Calories: 330; Protein: 13.14; Fat: 14.57; Carbs: 38.04

Caprese Stuffed Chicken Breast

Prep Time: 15 mins
Cook Time: 25 mins
Servings: 4

Ingredients:

- 4 boneless, skinless chicken breasts
- 4 slices mozzarella cheese
- 4 slices tomato
- 4 large basil leaves
- 2 tablespoons balsamic glaze
- Salt and pepper to taste
- Olive oil for cooking

Directions:

1. Preheat the oven to 400°F.
2. Using a sharp knife, make a horizontal slit in each chicken breast to create a pocket.
3. Season the chicken breasts with salt and pepper.
4. Place a slice of mozzarella cheese, a slice of tomato, and a basil leaf inside each pocket.
5. Secure the pockets closed with toothpicks.
6. Heat olive oil in an oven-safe skillet over medium-high heat.
7. Add the stuffed chicken breasts to the skillet and cook for 2-3 minutes per side, until browned.
8. Transfer the skillet to the preheated oven and bake for 15-20 minutes, or until the chicken is cooked through and the cheese is melted and bubbly.
9. Remove from the oven and let the chicken rest for a few minutes.
10. Drizzle the balsamic glaze over the chicken breasts before serving. Serve hot.

Nutritional Value (Amount per Serving):

Calories: 96; Protein: 8.69; Fat: 4.95; Carbs: 4.82

Orange Ginger Glazed Chicken

Prep Time: 15 mins
Cook Time: 25 mins
Servings: 4

Ingredients:

- 4 boneless, skinless chicken breasts
- 1/4 cup orange juice
- 2 tablespoons soy sauce
- 2 tablespoons honey
- 1 tablespoon grated fresh ginger
- 2 cloves garlic, minced
- 1 teaspoon cornstarch
- 1 tablespoon vegetable oil
- Sesame seeds for garnish (optional)
- Sliced green onions for garnish (optional)

Directions:

1. In a small bowl, whisk together the orange juice, soy sauce, honey, grated ginger, minced garlic, and cornstarch. Set aside.
2. Heat the vegetable oil in a large skillet over medium-high heat.
3. Season the chicken breasts with salt and pepper.
4. Add the chicken breasts to the skillet and cook for 5-6 minutes per side, or until browned and cooked through.
5. Pour the orange ginger glaze over the chicken in the skillet.
6. Cook for an additional 2-3 minutes, or until the glaze thickens and coats the chicken.
7. Remove from heat and garnish with sesame seeds and sliced green onions if desired. Serve hot.

Nutritional Value (Amount per Serving):

Calories: 100; Protein: 0.85; Fat: 4.88; Carbs: 14.02

Creamy Mushroom Chicken Skillet

Prep Time: 15 mins
Cook Time: 25 mins
Servings: 4

Ingredients:

- 4 boneless, skinless chicken breasts
- 2 tablespoons olive oil
- 8 ounces mushrooms, sliced
- 2 cloves garlic, minced
- 1 cup chicken broth
- 1 cup heavy cream
- 1 teaspoon dried thyme
- 1/2 teaspoon dried rosemary
- Fresh parsley for garnish (optional)
- Salt and pepper to taste

Directions:

1. Season the chicken breasts with salt and pepper.
2. Heat the olive oil in a large skillet over medium-high heat.
3. Add the chicken breasts to the skillet and cook for 5-6 minutes per side, or until browned and cooked through. Remove the chicken from the skillet and set aside.
4. In the same skillet, add the sliced mushrooms and minced garlic. Cook for 5 minutes, or until the mushrooms are tender and golden brown.
5. Pour the chicken broth into the skillet and bring to a simmer.
6. Stir in the heavy cream, dried thyme, and dried rosemary. Cook for 5 minutes, or until the sauce thickens slightly.
7. Return the cooked chicken breasts to the skillet and simmer for an additional 2-3 minutes, or until the chicken is heated through and coated with the creamy mushroom sauce.
8. Remove from heat and garnish with fresh parsley if desired. Serve hot.

Nutritional Value (Amount per Serving):

Calories: 278; Protein: 15.67; Fat: 22.23; Carbs: 4.78

Chapter 7: Snacks

Recipe Title: Protein-Packed Energy Bites

Prep Time: 15 mins
Chill Time: 1 hour
Servings: 12

Ingredients:

- 1 cup old-fashioned rolled oats
- ½ cup peanut butter
- ¼ cup honey
- ¼ cup chocolate chips
- ¼ cup ground flaxseed
- 2 tablespoons chia seeds
- 1 teaspoon vanilla extract

Directions:

1. In a large mixing bowl, combine oats, peanut butter, honey, chocolate chips, ground flaxseed, chia seeds, and vanilla extract.
2. Stir well until all the Ingredients: are evenly combined.
3. Cover the bowl and refrigerate for 1 hour to allow the mixture to firm up.
4. Once chilled, remove from the refrigerator and shape the mixture into 12 bite-sized balls.
5. Store the energy bites in an airtight container in the refrigerator for up to one week.

Nutritional Value (Amount per Serving):

Calories: 91; Protein: 2.77; Fat: 3.95; Carbs: 14.71

Veggie Pinwheels

Prep Time: 20 mins
Chill Time: 2 hours
Servings: 8

Ingredients:

- 4 large flour tortillas
- 8 ounces cream cheese, softened
- 1 cup shredded carrots
- 1 cup baby spinach leaves
- ½ cup diced red bell pepper
- ½ cup diced cucumber

Direction :

1. Lay the flour tortillas flat on a clean surface.
2. Spread an even layer of cream cheese over each tortilla.
3. Sprinkle shredded carrots, baby spinach leaves, diced red bell pepper, and diced cucumber evenly over the cream cheese.
4. Starting from one end, tightly roll up each tortilla into a log shape.
5. Wrap each rolled tortilla in plastic wrap and refrigerate for at least 2 hours to allow them to set.
6. Once chilled, remove the plastic wrap and slice each tortilla log into 1-inch pinwheels.
7. Serve the veggie pinwheels as a healthy snack or appetizer.

Nutritional Value (Amount per Serving):

Calories: 161; Protein: 4.21; Fat: 9.55; Carbs: 14.9

Greek Yogurt Parfait

Prep Time: 5 mins
Total Time: 10 mins
Servings: 1

Ingredients:

- ½ cup Greek yogurt
- ¼ cup granola
- ¼ cup mixed berries (strawberries, blueberries, raspberries)
- 1 tablespoon honey

Directions:

1. In a glass or bowl, layer half of the Greek yogurt.
2. Sprinkle half of the granola over the yogurt.
3. Add half of the mixed berries on top of the granola.
4. Drizzle half of the honey over the berries.
5. Repeat the layers with the remaining Ingredients:.
6. Serve the Greek yogurt parfait immediately or refrigerate for later.

Nutritional Value (Amount per Serving):

Calories: 64; Protein: 0.06; Fat: 0; Carbs: 17.3

Quinoa Salad Cups

Prep Time: 20 mins
Cook Time: 15 mins
Servings: 6

Ingredients:

- 1 cup cooked quinoa
- ½ cup diced cucumber
- ½ cup diced tomatoes
- ½ cup diced bell peppers (assorted colors)
- ¼ cup chopped fresh parsley
- 2 tablespoons olive oil
- 2 tablespoons lemon juice
- Salt and pepper to taste
- 6 lettuce leaves (such as romaine or butter lettuce)

Directions:

1. In a large mixing bowl, combine cooked quinoa, diced cucumber, diced tomatoes, diced bell peppers, chopped fresh parsley, olive oil, lemon juice, salt, and pepper.
2. Mix well to ensure all the Ingredients: are evenly coated.
3. Place a lettuce leaf in each serving cup or container.
4. Spoon the quinoa salad into each lettuce cup, dividing it evenly.
5. Serve the quinoa salad cups immediately or refrigerate until ready to eat.

Nutritional Value (Amount per Serving):

Calories: 87; Protein: 1.84; Fat: 5.19; Carbs: 8.84

Baked Sweet Potato Chips

Prep Time: 10 mins
Cook Time: 20 mins
Servings: 4

Ingredients:

- 2 large sweet potatoes
- 2 tablespoons olive oil
- 1 teaspoon paprika
- ½ teaspoon salt
- ¼ teaspoon black pepper

Directions:

1. Preheat the oven to 400°F and line a baking sheet with parchment paper.
2. Wash and dry the sweet potatoes, then slice them into thin rounds using a sharp knife or a mandoline slicer.
3. In a large bowl, combine olive oil, paprika, salt, and black pepper.
4. Add the sweet potato slices to the bowl and toss them until evenly coated with the oil and spice mixture.
5. Arrange the coated sweet potato slices in a single layer on the prepared baking sheet.
6. Bake in the preheated oven for 20 minutes, flipping the chips halfway through, until they are crispy and golden brown.
7. Remove from the oven and let the sweet potato chips cool completely before serving.

Nutritional Value (Amount per Serving):

Calories: 143; Protein: 1.91; Fat: 6.96; Carbs: 19.06

Caprese Skewers

Prep Time: 15 mins
Total Time: 15 mins
Servings: 12 skewers

Ingredients:

- 24 cherry tomatoes
- 12 small mozzarella balls
- 12 fresh basil leaves
- 2 tablespoons balsamic glaze
- Salt and pepper to taste
- 12 skewers (wooden or metal)

Directions:

1. Thread a cherry tomato onto a skewer, followed by a mozzarella ball and a fresh basil leaf.
2. Repeat the process for the remaining skewers, alternating the ingredients.
3. Arrange the caprese skewers on a serving platter.
4. Drizzle balsamic glaze over the skewers.
5. Season with salt and pepper to taste.
6. Serve the caprese skewers immediately or refrigerate until ready to serve.

Nutritional Value (Amount per Serving):

Calories: 5; Protein: 0.3; Fat: 0.05; Carbs: 1.13

Apple Cinnamon Muffins

Prep Time: 15 mins
Cook Time: 20 mins
Servings: 12

Ingredients:

- 2 cups all-purpose flour
- 2 teaspoons baking powder
- 1 teaspoon ground cinnamon
- ½ teaspoon salt
- ½ cup unsalted butter, melted
- 1 cup milk
- 2 large eggs
- 1 teaspoon vanilla extract
- 1 apple, peeled, cored, and diced
- 1 cup granulated sugar

Directions:

1. Preheat the oven to 375°F and line a muffin tin with paper liners.
2. In a large mixing bowl, combine flour, sugar, baking powder, ground cinnamon, and salt.
3. In a separate bowl, whisk together melted butter, milk, eggs, and vanilla extract.
4. Pour the wet Ingredients: into the dry Ingredients: and stir until just combined.
5. Fold in the diced apple.
6. Divide the batter evenly among the prepared muffin cups, filling each about 2/3 full.
7. Bake in the preheated oven for 18-20 minutes, or until a toothpick inserted into the center of a muffin comes out clean.
8. Remove from the oven and let the muffins cool in the tin for a few minutes before transferring them to a wire rack to cool completely.

Nutritional Value (Amount per Serving):

Calories: 186; Protein: 3.6; Fat: 6.79; Carbs: 27.6

Antipasto Skewers

Prep Time: 20 mins
Total Time: 15 mins
Servings: 12 skewers

Ingredients:

- 12 cherry tomatoes
- 12 small mozzarella balls
- 12 slices salami
- 12 pitted black olives
- 12 marinated artichoke hearts
- 12 skewers (wooden or metal)

Directions:

1. Thread a cherry tomato onto a skewer, followed by a mozzarella ball, a slice of salami folded into quarters, a black olive, and a marinated artichoke heart.
2. Repeat the process for the remaining skewers, alternating the ingredients.
3. Arrange the antipasto skewers on a serving platter.
4. Serve the antipasto skewers immediately or refrigerate until ready to serve.

Nutritional Value (Amount per Serving):

Calories: 178; Protein: 11.43; Fat: 8.05; Carbs: 18.92

Trail Mix Bars

Prep Time: 15 mins
Chill Time: 1 hour
Servings: 12

Ingredients:

- 2 cups rolled oats
- 1 cup peanut butter
- ½ cup honey
- ½ cup mixed nuts (almonds, cashews, peanuts), chopped
- ½ cup dried cranberries
- ¼ cup mini chocolate chips
- 1 teaspoon vanilla extract

Directions:

1. Line an 8x8-inch baking dish with parchment paper.
2. In a large mixing bowl, combine rolled oats, peanut butter, honey, mixed nuts, dried cranberries, mini chocolate chips, and vanilla extract.
3. Stir well until all the ingredients are evenly combined.
4. Transfer the mixture to the prepared baking dish and press it down firmly using the back of a spoon or your hands.
5. Refrigerate for at least 1 hour to allow the bars to set.
6. Once chilled, remove from the refrigerator and cut into 12 bars.
7. Store the trail mix bars in an airtight container in the refrigerator for up to one week.

Nutritional Value (Amount per Serving):

Calories: 184; Protein: 5.53; Fat: 7.93; Carbs: 30.05

Cucumber Sushi Rolls

Prep Time: 10 mins
Total Time: 10 mins
Servings: 4

Ingredients:

- 4 large cucumbers
- ½ cup cooked sushi rice
- ¼ cup sliced avocado
- ¼ cup sliced carrots
- ¼ cup sliced red bell pepper
- ¼ cup sliced cucumber
- 4 sheets nori (seaweed)

Directions:

1. Cut the cucumbers lengthwise into thin, flat slices using a vegetable peeler or a mandoline slicer.
2. Lay a sheet of nori flat on a clean surface.
3. Place cucumber slices on the nori, slightly overlapping, to create a rectangular shape.
4. Spread a thin layer of sushi rice over the cucumber slices.
5. Arrange avocado, carrots, red bell pepper, and cucumber slices on top of the rice.
6. Starting from one end, tightly roll up the nori and filling into a sushi roll.
7. Repeat the process for the remaining Ingredients:.
8. Slice each sushi roll into bite-sized pieces.
9. Serve the cucumber sushi rolls with soy sauce or your favorite dipping sauce.

Nutritional Value (Amount per Serving):

Calories: 97; Protein: 4.02; Fat: 4.91; Carbs: 14.61

Buffalo Cauliflower Bites

Prep Time: 15 mins
Cook Time: 20 mins
Servings: 4

Ingredients:

- 1 small head cauliflower, cut into florets
- ½ cup milk
- 1 teaspoon garlic powder
- ½ teaspoon salt
- ¼ teaspoon black pepper
- ¼ cup hot sauce
- 2 tablespoons unsalted butter, melted
- ½ cup all-purpose flour

Directions:

1. Preheat the oven to 450°F and line a baking sheet with parchment paper.
2. In a large mixing bowl, whisk together flour, milk, garlic powder, salt, and black pepper until smooth.
3. Add cauliflower florets to the bowl and toss them until evenly coated with the batter.
4. Arrange the coated cauliflower florets in a single layer on the prepared baking sheet.
5. Bake in the preheated oven for 15 minutes, flipping the florets halfway through.
6. In a separate bowl, combine hot sauce and melted butter.
7. Remove the cauliflower florets from the oven and brush them with the hot sauce mixture.
8. Return the baking sheet to the oven and bake for an additional 5 minutes, until the cauliflower is crispy and lightly browned.
9. Remove from the oven and let the buffalo cauliflower bites cool for a few minutes before serving.

Nutritional Value (Amount per Serving):

Calories: 132; Protein: 4.3; Fat: 5.26; Carbs: 17.6

Chapter 8: Sauces, Dressings & Staples

Tangy Lemon Vinaigrette

Prep Time: 5 mins
Total Time: 10 mins
Servings: 4

Ingredients:

- ¼ cup freshly squeezed lemon juice
- ¼ cup olive oil
- 1 tablespoon Dijon mustard
- 1 teaspoon honey
- Salt and pepper to taste

Directions:

1. In a small bowl, whisk together lemon juice, olive oil, Dijon mustard, and honey until well combined.
2. Season with salt and pepper to taste.
3. Use immediately as a salad dressing or store in an airtight container in the refrigerator for up to one week.

Nutritional Value (Amount per Serving):

Calories: 135; Protein: 0.43; Fat: 13.69; Carbs: 3.81

Creamy Avocado Sauce

Prep Time: 10 mins
Total Time: 15 mins
Servings: 4

Ingredients:

- 1 ripe avocado, peeled and pitted
- ¼ cup Greek yogurt
- 2 tablespoons freshly squeezed lime juice
- 2 tablespoons chopped fresh cilantro
- 1 clove garlic, minced
- Salt and pepper to taste

Directions:

1. In a blender or food processor, combine avocado, Greek yogurt, lime juice, cilantro, and garlic.
2. Blend until smooth and creamy.
3. Season with salt and pepper to taste.
4. Use as a sauce for tacos, burritos, or as a dip for vegetables.

Nutritional Value (Amount per Serving):

Calories: 88; Protein: 1.32; Fat: 7.4; Carbs: 6.25

Spicy Sriracha Mayo

Prep Time: 5 mins
Total Time: 10 mins
Servings: 4

Ingredients:

- ½ cup mayonnaise
- 1 tablespoon Sriracha sauce
- 1 teaspoon lime juice
- ½ teaspoon garlic powder

Directions:

1. In a small bowl, whisk together mayonnaise, Sriracha sauce, lime juice, and garlic powder until well combined.
2. Adjust the amount of Sriracha sauce to your desired level of spiciness.
3. Use as a dipping sauce for fries, sushi, or as a spread for sandwiches.

Nutritional Value (Amount per Serving):

Calories: 100; Protein: 1.93; Fat: 9.55; Carbs: 1.62

Balsamic Glaze

Prep Time: 5 mins
Cook Time: 15 mins
Servings: 4

Ingredients:

- 1 cup balsamic vinegar
- 2 tablespoons honey

Directions:

1. In a small saucepan, combine balsamic vinegar and honey.
2. Bring the mixture to a boil over medium heat.
3. Reduce the heat to low and simmer for about 15 minutes, or until the mixture has thickened and reduced by half.
4. Remove from heat and let it cool.
5. Use the balsamic glaze as a drizzle for salads, roasted vegetables, or grilled meats.

Nutritional Value (Amount per Serving):

Calories: 88; Protein: 0.34; Fat: 0; Carbs: 19.51

Honey Mustard Dressing

Prep Time: 5 mins
Total Time: 10 mins
Servings: 4

Ingredients:

- ¼ cup Dijon mustard
- 2 tablespoons honey
- 2 tablespoons apple cider vinegar
- 2 tablespoons olive oil
- Salt and pepper to taste

Directions:

1. In a small bowl, whisk together Dijon mustard, honey, apple cider vinegar, and olive oil until well combined.
2. Season with salt and pepper to taste.
3. Use as a dressing for salads or as a dipping sauce for chicken tenders or vegetables.

Nutritional Value (Amount per Serving):

Calories: 107; Protein: 0.84; Fat: 7.29; Carbs: 10.69

Creamy Garlic Parmesan Sauce

Prep Time: 10 mins
Cook Time: 5 mins
Servings: 4

Ingredients:

- 1 tablespoon butter
- 2 cloves garlic, minced
- 1 cup heavy cream
- ½ cup grated Parmesan cheese
- Salt and pepper to taste
- Chopped fresh parsley for garnish

Directions:

1. In a saucepan, melt butter over medium heat.
2. Add minced garlic and sauté for about 1 minute, until fragrant.
3. Stir in heavy cream and bring to a simmer.
4. Reduce heat to low and whisk in grated Parmesan cheese until melted and smooth.
5. Season with salt and pepper to taste.
6. Remove from heat and garnish with chopped fresh parsley.
7. Serve the creamy garlic Parmesan sauce over pasta, grilled chicken, or roasted vegetables.

Nutritional Value (Amount per Serving):

Calories: 194; Protein: 4.96; Fat: 17.61; Carbs: 5.09

Teriyaki Sauce

Prep Time: 5 mins
Cook Time: 10 mins
Servings: 4

Ingredients:

- ½ cup soy sauce
- ¼ cup water
- 2 tablespoons brown sugar
- 1 tablespoon honey
- 1 tablespoon rice vinegar
- 1 clove garlic, minced
- 1 teaspoon grated fresh ginger
- 1 tablespoon cornstarch
- 1 tablespoon water

Directions:

1. In a small saucepan, combine soy sauce, water, brown sugar, honey, rice vinegar, minced garlic, and grated ginger.
2. Bring the mixture to a simmer over medium heat.
3. In a separate bowl, whisk together cornstarch and water to make a slurry.
4. Slowly pour the slurry into the saucepan while whisking continuously.
5. Continue to simmer the sauce, stirring constantly, until it thickens to your desired consistency.
6. Remove from heat and let it cool.
7. Use the teriyaki sauce as a glaze for grilled meats, a marinade for chicken or tofu, or as a dipping sauce for sushi or spring rolls.

Nutritional Value (Amount per Serving):

Calories: 134; Protein: 2.35; Fat: 5.78; Carbs: 18.44

Cilantro Lime Dressing

Prep Time: 5 mins
Total Time: 10 mins
Servings: 4
Ingredients:

- ½ cup Greek yogurt
- ¼ cup freshly squeezed lime juice
- 2 tablespoons chopped fresh cilantro
- 1 clove garlic, minced
- 1 tablespoon honey
- Salt and pepper to taste

Directions:

1. In a blender or food processor, combine Greek yogurt, lime juice, cilantro, minced garlic, and honey.
2. Blend until smooth and creamy.
3. Season with salt and pepper to taste.
4. Use as a dressing for salads or as a sauce for tacos or grilled chicken.

Nutritional Value (Amount per Serving):

Calories: 25; Protein: 0.36; Fat: 0.04; Carbs: 6.93

Peanut Sauce

Prep Time: 5 mins
Cook Time: 5 mins
Servings: 4

Ingredients:

- ½ cup creamy peanut butter
- 2 tablespoons soy sauce
- 2 tablespoons rice vinegar
- 1 tablespoon honey
- 1 clove garlic, minced
- 1 teaspoon grated fresh ginger
- ¼ cup water

Directions:

1. In a small saucepan, combine peanut butter, soy sauce, rice vinegar, honey, minced garlic, and grated ginger.
2. Heat the mixture over low heat, stirring constantly, until the peanut butter has melted and the sauce is smooth.
3. Stir in water to thin the sauce to your desired consistency.
4. Remove from heat and let it cool.
5. Use the peanut sauce as a dip for spring rolls, a dressing for noodle salads, or as a sauce for stir-fried vegetables.

Nutritional Value (Amount per Serving):

Calories: 237; Protein: 8.47; Fat: 18.78; Carbs: 12.15

Roasted Red Pepper Sauce

Prep Time: 10 mins
Cook Time: 20 mins
Servings: 4

Ingredients:

- 2 large red bell peppers
- 2 tablespoons olive oil
- 1 clove garlic, minced
- ¼ cup tomato paste
- ¼ cup vegetable broth
- 1 tablespoon balsamic vinegar
- Salt and pepper to taste

Directions:

1. Preheat the broiler in your oven.
2. Cut the red bell peppers in half and remove the seeds and stems.
3. Place the pepper halves on a baking sheet, cut side down.
4. Broil the peppers for about 10 minutes, or until the skins are charred and blistered.
5. Remove the peppers from the oven and let them cool.
6. Once cooled, peel off the charred skins and discard.
7. In a blender or food processor, combine the roasted red peppers, olive oil, minced garlic, tomato paste, vegetable broth, and balsamic vinegar.
8. Blend until smooth and creamy.
9. Season with salt and pepper to taste.
10. Use the roasted red pepper sauce as a spread for sandwiches, a sauce for pasta, or as a dip for vegetables.

Nutritional Value (Amount per Serving):

Calories: 92; Protein: 1.46; Fat: 6.9; Carbs: 7.43

APPENDIX RECIPE INDEX

Printed in Great Britain
by Amazon

29738983R00064